THE
FEMALE
FEW

THE
FEMALE
FEW

SPITFIRE
HEROINES

JACKY HYAMS

This book is dedicated to the memory of the people of the Air Transport Auxiliary who sustained the Royal Air Force and the Fleet Air Arm during the Second World War.

'Remember then that also we, in a moon's course, are history'

(From the poem 'Passage' by John Drinkwater, inscribed on the ATA Memorial in the crypt at St Paul's Cathedral, London.)

'Some people, both sexes, didn't make it. They dropped out. There's a lot to flying. You need "the touch". I think women were much better when it came to flying the Spitfires. Women have a lighter touch. They're not as ham-fisted.'

(Yvonne MacDonald)

First published 2012
This paperback edition published 2016

The History Press
The Mill, Brimscombe Port
Stroud, Gloucestershire, GL5 2QG
www.thehistorypress.co.uk

© Jacky Hyams, 2012, 2016

The right of Jacky Hyams to be identified as the Author
of this work has been asserted in accordance with the
Copyright, Designs and Patents Act 1988.

British Library Cataloguing in Publication Data.
A catalogue record for this book is available from the British Library.

ISBN 978 0 7509 6818 8

Typesetting and origination by The History Press
Printed and bound by CPI Group (UK) Ltd

CONTENTS

FOREWORD

The story of the Air Transport Auxiliary is one of the most inspiring of the Second World War. It is an almost unbelievable tale of courage, skill and sacrifice. I first came across the Air Transport Auxiliary (ATA) in 1990, when I was researching an exhibition about the aviation history of Maidenhead. As a commercial pilot, I was awestruck and my interest in this forgotten story grew from that point on, encouraged by the fact that ATA's headquarters had been just outside Maidenhead at White Waltham, which is still an active airfield. Subsequently, in 1993, I was one of the team that set up and launched the Maidenhead Heritage Centre, of which I have been the Chairman since 1995.

Over the years, we have built up an impressive collection of historical ATA material, which we believe is the largest outside the Imperial War Museum and the RAF Museum at Hendon in North London. HRH Prince Michael of Kent opened Maidenhead Heritage Centre's dedicated ATA exhibition and archive in 2011 and it is already a centre of excellence for research into ATA, located 2 miles – or 30 seconds away by Spitfire – from White Waltham airfield.

Women taking to the skies was not new when the Second World War broke out. In 1910, Orville Wright's sister, Katherine, became the first woman in the world to fly and, a year later, Hilda Hewlett became the first woman to receive a British pilot's licence. The trail-blazing pioneers of aviation in the 1920s and 1930s included wonderful people like Lady Mary Bailey, Amy Johnson and the US aviator Amelia Earhart. These pilots caught the public imagination like no other before them. When Amy Johnson flew to Australia in 1930, Britain and Australia went crazy.

Pauline Gower, Head of the Women's Section of the ATA, was one of the most prominent women in aviation in the pre-war period. She was unusual in that she made her living out of flying, joyriding in the flying circuses. When she was asked, before the war, 'If there's a war, women won't be able to fly, will they?' Pauline's response set the tone for what was to happen. 'Why not?' she asked. Flying might have been seen as a man's world but her reply was spot on. There are no skills for flying that are inherently exclusive to men. So, for the women who flew for the ATA, there was nothing special about it.

Margaret Frost said she didn't care what the men thought. She just wanted to fly. She was a pilot and had a job to do; her gender was irrelevant. Initially, it was the Establishment that had the problem, despite the precedent of women flying in the 1920s and 1930s. One of the most interesting aspects of the story is that through the quiet diplomacy of Pauline Gower the basic principle of women in the ATA was conceded in the autumn of 1939, despite the resistance of certain sections of the Establishment. Then it was really a case of fighting for equality of opportunity and pay. The first women were restricted to flying trainer and communications aircraft, but in July 1941 Winifred Crossley became the first woman to be cleared to fly fighters. Then the sky was the limit and in 1943 a few women were at last permitted to fly four-engined bombers such as the Lancaster. In May that year the politically astute Pauline Gower won equal pay for the ladies of ATA, which thus became one of the first 'equal opportunity employers'.

People often marvel at the fact that the ferry pilots flew in the ever-changing British weather without radios or navigation aids, in the days before SatNav. Flight instruments showed how fast or high they were flying. However, because ATA pilots were required to stay within sight of the ground, they were not taught the art of flying on instruments – flying blind. Nevertheless many ATA pilots did teach themselves instrument flying, sometimes by scrounging sessions in a Link Trainer, a kind of rudimentary flight simulator. Flight above cloud was not permitted, though sometimes practised, simply because without radios there was no way for a pilot to find his or her way back down through the cloud. In time of war, radio silence was the order of the day, except for combat missions, whilst the radios themselves were pretty unsophisticated and the crystals needed changing all the time. Only when ATA started flying into Europe after D-Day in 1944 were its pilots given courses in how to use radios. Their call-sign was 'Ferdinand the Bull'.

Planning each day's work was a logistical nightmare. Each day, Central Ferry Control at Andover, Hampshire, would pass details of the next day's movements to the individual Ferry Pools. There, the operations officers worked out the most efficient way of using their available pilots. This might involve using air taxis to take the pilots to and from jobs.

The plane came out of the factory in a flyable but possibly unfinished state, sometimes with radios, armaments and some secondary instruments still to be fitted. So the ATA ferry pilot would arrive at the factory to fly the brand-new plane to a maintenance unit, generally in the west of the country – as far from enemy bombers as possible. When the plane was completed, another civilian pilot was sent by Ferry Control to fly it to the front line squadron, which could be anywhere in the UK.

So before the boys in blue got to see this shiny new plane, it had already been flown twice by an 'amateur'. Then the plane would go into battle and perhaps be damaged or need overhauling. So another civilian pilot would take it to a repair or maintenance unit, while yet another would deliver the serviceable plane to keep the squadron up to strength. In some cases, you could have the same plane being flown three, four or even more times by an ATA ferry pilot.

ATA work was dangerous. Some ferry pilots were shot at by the enemy and occasionally by their own side. But weather was the biggest hazard. Getting 'stuck out', in a location far from base, was not uncommon. Often, pilots would have to turn back or land if conditions were too bad. Yet the casualty rate among ATA women was proportionally much lower than amongst ATA men. One of the reasons is that the women were more reliable, tending to obey the rules more readily than some of the wilder elements amongst the men. Of course, there were always exceptions. One American woman told me: 'I flew across the airfield at a height of 10ft at 300 miles an hour!' Another frightened herself flying a Spitfire under a railway bridge across the Severn Estuary when the tide was in.

Perhaps ATA's women were more cautious because at the back of their minds they knew that people were looking over their shoulders, looking for any excuse to say: 'I told you women couldn't do it,' though I very much doubt if anyone ever said it to their faces.

These modest ladies often insist they were not 'special', that they were just doing their job. But they *were* special, along with their male colleagues, because they did such extraordinary things. To us, in a world of regulation, licences and certificates, the idea of flying six different types of plane in one day is unbelievable, particularly when you consider that they would be seeing some of those planes for the very first time. Nowadays it just would not be allowed to happen.

Interest in the ATA is high partly because the Second World War is still – just – in living memory. And although this should not be the case, there is something exciting about women achieving in what has traditionally been a man's world. Like it or not, there is a romance about the little woman against the elements, flying a Lancaster bomber or a Spitfire.

After the Second World War, many ATA women of course married and became mothers and homemakers. Of the women in this book, only Mary (Wilkins) Ellis stayed in aviation for the rest of her life. A few women, including Margaret Frost, Diana Barnato Walker and Freydis Leaf, continued to fly in the Women's Voluntary Reserve or the Women's Junior Air Corps and maintain a partial involvement with aviation. Generally this was with light aircraft and did not represent an aviation career, although Jackie Moggridge became a commercial airline pilot and Lettice Curtis worked for an aviation manufacturer as a senior flight development engineer. She could have been a test pilot but that just wasn't the kind of thing women did in the 1950s and 1960s. Joan Hughes, who died in 1993, worked as a flight instructor with West London Aero Club and the Airways Aero Association and flew vintage planes in two 1960s movies, *Those Magnificent Men in Their Flying Machines* and *Thunderbird 6*.

The contribution of the women of ATA to victory by keeping the RAF and Fleet Air Arm supplied with aircraft cannot be overestimated. I hope that this book will help us all to appreciate their amazing story of courage, skill and sacrifice.

Richard Poad MBE
Chairman of Maidenhead Heritage Centre
'The spiritual home of ATA'

INTRODUCTION

It was an unbelievably glamorous image. Such is the power of the single picture; it lifted hearts and spirits everywhere in the autumn of 1944 as it was picked up from the newsstands to be read on the way to work or in millions of blacked-out homes.

War weary families gazed in awe at the cover of *Picture Post* magazine and the black and white shot of a good looking woman, parachute on her shoulder, fingers running through hair streaming behind her in the sun, young, free – and in control of a mighty war machine, a Fairey Barracuda. Here was a female pilot, one of an elite group of civilian women who were helping Britain win the war. *Picture Post*, the most popular weekly magazine of the era, frequently published the outstanding visual images of wartime. And, of course, without television, such images had huge national impact.

The young woman, 1st Officer Maureen Dunlop, was part of an elite group of female flyers, women who had joined the civilian organisation, ATA (Air Transport Auxiliary) to carry out a dangerous but crucial wartime role: as a ferry pilot delivering new aircraft from the factories where they were being produced to the frontline squadrons on the RAF bases all over Britain, or ferrying damaged aircraft to and fro between factories, repair shops and RAF airfields.

The work was dangerous. ATA ferry pilots flew by day and did not intentionally face combat, though if they were unlucky enough to encounter a German fighter the result could be fatal. Through the war, sixteen female and 157 male ferry pilots working for the ATA lost their lives. Their 300,000-plus safe deliveries of all types of planes – from light trainers to four-engine bombers – made a heroic and substantial contribution to Britain's war effort. As civilian flyers, their work freed up the air force pilots to get on with the business of combat.

Each carefully planned delivery was a result of a complex schedule. The flying itself was perilous work: they flew unarmed, usually without radio, often without fully functioning navigation instruments. Ferry pilots had to cope with barrage balloons and unpredictable British weather (especially uncomfortable when flying in open cockpits in the early war years and life threatening if they flew into heavy cloud). At times, they would be flying in aircraft they had never flown before, relying on printed but very detailed notes to guide them through the hazards. Every single delivery counted. In a sense, they were 'backroom boys and girls', ensuring the RAF had what they needed, when they needed it. But without the ATA's valiant efforts, history might have been different.

The mythopoeic power of that *Picture Post* glamorous photo at the time was such that some even started to believe that it was only women pilots who were carrying out this all important work. In fact, the civilian female flyers of the ATA were a minority group. At the beginning of the war, in January 1940, the first civilian ferry pilots' pool consisted of just eight female pilots, experienced flyers, all with more than 600 flying hours, some of them with well over 1000 flying hours behind them. And while pioneering British aviators like Beryl Markham, Jean Batten and Amy Johnson – who lost her life in bad weather in 1941 while on a flying mission for the ATA – had started to make their mark on the world in the 1920s and 1930s, the female component of the ATA was small.

The ATA was certainly a diverse group of individuals. Men and women from over 25 different nationalities and from all walks of life took to the skies for the ATA as ferry pilots. At one stage the ATA was dubbed 'The Foreign Legion of the air' because so many different countries were represented.

'Ancient and Tattered Airmen' was another nickname, given because the men who flew for the ATA were those who did not fulfil the physical or age criteria needed to join the RAF and, in some instances, the men were disabled or veterans of the First World War.

The eventual number of women who flew for the ATA through Second World War was just 168 – out of 1245 ATA pilots and flight engineers. And they were superbly backed up: at its peak in August 1944, the ATA also deployed some 2786 civilian ground staff. Ferrying planes from A to B in wartime Britain was a supreme test of logistics and planning: so the operations officers, ground engineers, office and medical staff, drivers, messengers and pilots' assistants of the ATA all had their important role to play.

Yet it was bound to be the women pilots who captured the wider public imagination, hungry as people were for any glimpse of stardust to distract them from the wartime gloom. Right from the start of the war, in January 1940 when newspaper articles and photos of those first eight women started to appear on breakfast tables across the country, it was clear that an exceptional group of skilled women pilots were boldly striking out, action women in the mould of Earhart and Johnson. Theirs became the glamour, the glory of the smart tailored uniform, the bold gold stripes to denote rank and, of course, the very idea that women were cheerfully and capably doing what was very much seen to be a man's job – flying.

Our fascination with 'the female few', the handful of women who flew Spitfires, Hurricanes, Barracudas, Harvards, Wellington Bombers, Lancasters and more across Britain's troubled skies in those six years, remains undiminished. Over 70 years since the

Second World War ended, the allure of their wartime adventure lives on. Commercial aviation itself has lost much of its original lustre, so we are still irresistibly drawn back to the Spitfire Women, as they are often known, up there in the skies, helping save Britain.

Part of the reason for this is that the Spitfire itself has, over time, become the superstar of wartime nostalgia. We see it as an important link with a time when a tiny, beleaguered country overcame the odds – and produced a superb fighter plane to help do it.

Built in greater numbers than any other British plane during wartime, the Spitfire has the distinction of being the only fighter to be continuously in production through the war years – though the advent of jets meant that by the time war ended, the 'Spit' was becoming obsolete.

Over 20,000 Spitfires were made for the RAF during the Second World War. At one point, one Spitfire factory at Castle Bromwich, near Birmingham, was manufacturing 320 Spitfires a month, ten a day. In the month of May 1944, Mary (Wilkins) Ellis' log notes 25 Spitfire deliveries from factory to base, sometimes ferrying three Spits in one day. Some have seen it in one way as a 'woman's plane'. 'You could dance with a Spitfire, it responded to the lightest touch,' said Molly Rose, who flew 36 different types of plane for the ATA through the war. Today, just a handful of Spitfires are left in the world. The memories of the remaining 'few' who lived to tell the tale and remain with us are becoming as valuable and rare as the legendary planes themselves (an airworthy Spitfire was reported to have sold for close to £2 million in 2009).

As a journalist, the Female Few entered my life courtesy of an excellent documentary on the BBC followed by a phone call from a publisher a few days later, asking me to look into the idea of interviewing some of the surviving ATA women pilots. Some fascinating books had been written about and by ATA female pilots over the years. A number of documentaries have also celebrated their work. Yet a small number of female ATA pilots were still alive and well. The idea was to interview them about their wartime work, certainly, but also to attempt to tell their personal stories, their individual lives before and since those days, in their own words.

Since 'what happened next?' is high on every journalist's agenda, this struck me as a most intriguing assignment. Who were these women? And what did life throw at them once they had made their last delivery and the ATA was disbanded?

I thought, more by instinct than research, that any surviving 'Few' who would be willing to tell me their stories would have put their flying days behind them for good as soon as the Second World War ended (I wasn't quite right on that one) but the opportunity to find out so much more about these women, their lives and their memories, was compelling. And here were important stories that needed to be told for posterity.

The five women I interviewed for this book retained the links with their past and the Air Transport Auxiliary. In a sense, they had already become aviation 'celebrities' in their own right, deserving all of the attention they were receiving in later life. Though age and distance were making it increasingly difficult for the surviving pilots to meet up with each other, an ATA reunion dinner in the autumn of 2011 meant I could initially meet Joy Lofthouse and Margaret Frost to introduce myself. Yes, they were happy to tell me their stories. By now, they had become experienced interviewees anyway. It was a good start. Clearly, their advancing years would be no barrier to the occasionally tiresome process of a series of interviews.

As the history of the ATA's early days includes the recruitment of a group of women from well-to-do backgrounds, I started out assuming that *all* my interviewees came from privileged, or upper class backgrounds and that was why they were able to indulge their passion for aviation in the first place. I wasn't quite right. Whilst the early war years saw civilian pilots with existing flying experience or training being recruited by the ATA, as time went on the need for more ferry pilots meant pilots, both sexes, were also being recruited without any flying experience, *ab initio* through magazine advertisements. Once recruited they were then trained from scratch.

So it came as a surprise to learn that some of the women did not fit the stereotype: the Gough Girls, Joy and Yvonne, as the young sisters were known locally in Cirencester, came from ordinary backgrounds, had never been near a plane before and wanted to fly because they were, like millions of other women, keen to make their individual contribution to the war effort.

Margaret Frost was a country parson's daughter who had carefully saved up her schoolgirl pocket money for flying lessons, much to the initial dismay of her family. Molly Rose and Mary (Wilkins) Ellis were, indeed, from comfortable backgrounds. Though their inherent modesty – a trait of all the women interviewed for this book and so typical of their generation – meant that they did not, quite clearly, view themselves as in any way different from anyone else or deserving of any special treatment.

As you might expect from people who were born in the early part of the twentieth century, while their memories of their wartime experiences were vivid and had left a powerful imprint on their subsequent lives, they had also encountered their own personal tragedies or setbacks. Yvonne MacDonald was already a young war widow and still grieving when she decided to apply to the ATA; but like many other bereaved women then, she was not about to let personal feelings prevent her from making her contribution to the war effort.

Clearly resilient and definitely not prone to hyperbole, each woman told me – insisted – that their ATA work meant doing a job, no more, no less, and that heroics or courage didn't come into it, this was simply the way it was, 'doing your bit for your country'. That was what millions of women did. Today, such reticence or understatement is uncommon. And the fact that they were, essentially, doing a man's job in wartime was, for them, something to smile about, rather than provoking any militancy or table thumping attitudes about women's roles or rights, either in aviation or peacetime.

As for all the attention they got in their smart tailored uniforms – all that perceived glamour for flyers, both sexes – it was not unwelcome. Why should it be? They were young and attractive women. But the inherent truth of it all was, they wanted to fly. The ATA motto: *Aetheris Avidi*, 'Eager for the Air' sums it up perfectly.

They also, in turn, expressed an essentially feminine common sense about their task: they were cautious in their approach to their work as ferry pilots. And they were, of course, constantly reminded of the wisdom of such an approach: 'We pay you to be safe, not brave' was the notice prominently displayed at the entrance to the Operations Section at Hamble, the all women's Ferry Pool. They might have been widely portrayed as adventurous daredevils in leather flying jackets and goggles, yet right from day one of their training, they were acutely conscious of the huge responsibility they undertook.

Being tasked with transporting these very expensive, often brand-new war machines from factory to base meant not making any mistakes. A daredevil, gung ho approach to flying was out of the question. Was that fear of crashing and loss of life? I asked them all in turn, knowing that one in ten ATA female ferry pilots lost their lives, though the women's fatality record was lower than that of the men. No, they all told me, the fear was not for themselves or their own survival. Their overall concern was not to thwart the war effort by damaging the aircraft in any way. You had to be extra careful. That was how you were trained.

One thing that also came out loud and clear to me through our interviews was that the language of their generation was totally different to the everyday language of the twenty-first century. Essentially, I was seeking their personal stories and memories. They were happy to answer every question. But understatement was, mostly, their style. Florid expressions of emotion – or displaying emotion – had never played a part in their world. The torrent of personal, intimate revelations we are bombarded with now, the finer detail of what it's like to experience shock, grief, pain is very much a hallmark of the times we live in now. It wasn't like that back then.

Beyond the physical difficulties or dangers of their flying, consider the day-to-day realities they sometimes faced on the ground: turning up for the day's work at the ferry pool to learn that a close friend, another female pilot, had been killed in an accident. Whilst working for the ATA, Molly Rose placed ads in *The Times* for news of her husband, missing in action, believed killed. Then she learned he was alive, but imprisoned. Yet even had she not received the good news, it is doubtful that she would have stopped flying. Many others had to fly knowing close family members were lost.

Certainly, intensely personal dramas like these were being experienced by millions all through the Second World War. And even now, sadly, our armed forces and their families must face the worst at times. Whilst due homage is now frequently made to the way the women of Britain coped courageously through wartime, whether they were dashing aviators or ordinary women, struggling to raise families as best they could, the way they all dealt with tragedy or wartime uncertainty transcended their backgrounds or individual circumstances: they didn't stop or collapse. They simply got on with it. They took in the truth of their situation and dealt with it as best they could. Histrionics or self pity were as unacceptable to the ATA women pilots as taking the slightest risk in the air. As Molly Rose put it: 'Everyone was doing their part for the war. Ours was just a more interesting job than most.'

You need a cool head to be a safe, capable pilot. And you need excellent co-ordination skills. Joy Lofthouse believed the athletic background she and her sister Yvonne shared gave them a real advantage when it came to being accepted as trainee pilots without experience. Mary (Wilkins) Ellis, a sickly infant, confidently took the controls and soared into the air in a Spitfire, aged 90. And there's the dogged determination factor too: Margaret Frost was rejected initially, told she did not quite fit the criteria. Yet eventually she was in the cockpit, safely ferrying Spitfires. So it is fair to say that their collective determination to do a good job, not take any risks, coupled with a resilient temperament or personality well suited to the times – where staying cool and calm was the only way to get through the worst – meant they could withstand what we now view as the awesome difficulties of their wartime role.

Today, we make so much of sharing our feelings, showing we care or how we feel. This generation were schooled completely differently: mostly, you kept such personal feelings to yourself. Spending time with these women made me understand very clearly, that the 'stiff upper lip' was not a cliché about the wartime British invented by Hollywood. It was real, the only sensible way to get through the worst times.

The American women who joined the ATA pilots later in the war were known to comment on this remarkable restraint. Frequently, silence was out of consideration for other people's feelings, knowing they too had their share of wartime concerns. There was no counselling or talking balm for sudden loss or bereavement. You got a day or two off the roster. Then you went back to the job. As Margaret Frost put it so succinctly: 'Feelings? We didn't have time for feelings. There was a war on.'

Recognition for these women and the work of the ATA took a long time to come. Whilst a memorial plaque was placed in the crypt of St Paul's Cathedral in London in 1950, commemorating the 173 men and women of the ATA who were killed serving in the organisation, the important role of the ATA women pilots themselves went largely unnoticed for decades. And it is fair to say they did not expect any kind of praise or acclaim.

Only in 2008 were the few surviving members presented with special award badges by the then Prime Minister, Gordon Brown, at 10 Downing Street after an ATA reunion at Maidenhead, near White Waltham, ATA's headquarters.

For anyone keen to learn more about the ATA, the Maidenhead Heritage Centre is a very good place to start, with its collection of ATA memorabilia and stories of its past. There have, of course, been several books written about the ATA, though some are no longer in print and require some diligent tracking down. Most notable of those available are *Spitfire Women of World War II* by Giles Whittell and *Spreading Their Wings* by the late Diana Barnato Walker. The late Lettice Curtis' book, *The Forgotten Pilots: A Story of the Air Transport Auxiliary 1939–45* is a very detailed history of the female flyers and their wartime work.

In my research I was fascinated to learn more about the ATA women who continued to fly after the war, so I have included short histories of several remarkable women in Appendix IV. I have also included an introductory brief history of the ATA's formation, the work of the women pilots and other key areas of interest until its disbandment in November 1945.

For families seeking more of their own personal history, there is a full list of the names of all the female ferry pilots who flew for the ATA. This book focusses on the five women who have told me their story, but it is intended as a tribute to every one of the ATA female flyers.

I would like to offer sincere thanks to those who were so helpful and generous to me with their time. Richard Poad, whose continuous hard work and dedication keep the ATA flame burning so brightly; the British Legion Press Office, whose initial assistance led me to Eric and Mary Viles (whose diligent work on behalf of the ATA Veterans' Association came as a result of Eric's wartime work as an Air Cadet/Pilot's Assistant from 1944–1945); and, of course, all gratitude and thanks to the remarkable Few. Molly Rose, Mary (Wilkins) Ellis, Joy Lofthouse, the late Yvonne MacDonald and Margaret Frost – inspirational, brave, modest women, so deserving of the attention that came to them late in life.

They have insisted repeatedly that all 'the Female Few' were just ordinary women 'doing their bit' like everyone else. Most of us, nevertheless, cannot help looking up and remembering all those fighter planes making their way across the stormy skies of war with a tinge of awe and wonder.

Jacky Hyams
East Sussex
2016

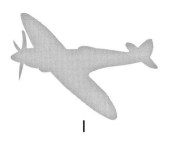

I

A Brief History

In the 1920s and 1930s, the idea of taking to the skies was growing in popularity. Flying clubs had already started up in the 1920s, partially subsidised by the British Government. It was not until October 1938, when it was clear to some that war was imminent, that the Civil Air Guard scheme was devised, thanks to the efforts of Gerard D'Erlanger, a director of the then British Overseas Airways Corporation and an enthusiastic private pilot. The idea of this scheme was to encourage civilian would-be flyers. They might well be needed if war broke out. The scheme offered subsidised flying lessons at flying clubs. It was widely available to civilians, either sex, ages 18–50, who passed the private pilot's 'A' licence medical.

The response to the news that the Government was contributing to flying lessons via the Civil Air Guard was overwhelming. Over 4000 would be flyers signed up. By May 1939, female members of the Civil Air Guard included approximately 200 pilots.

At that point, while the Parliamentary Under Secretary of State for Air had told the House of Commons that in a national emergency, civilian women would certainly be used to ferry aircraft, it remained unclear where or how they would be deployed. Would it be via the ATS (the Women's Army Auxiliary) or the WAAF (the Women's Auxiliary Air Force)? No decision was made.

When war finally broke out at the beginning of September 1939 it was still unclear what kind of role, if any, the civilian women pilots would be playing. Yet the Air Transport Auxiliary or ATA was formed – thanks again to the resourceful efforts of Gerard d'Erlanger, founder and Commanding Officer of the ATA. He had foreseen a shortage of trained pilots if the qualified civilian group who could fly were excluded from joining the RAF. And it had been agreed that civilian women pilots could fly, so they could fly for the ATA.

Gerard D'Erlanger initially saw the ATA as a courier service, flying VIPs and wounded servicemen. But it quickly became obvious that the role of these civilian pilots would extend beyond that – and would involve ferrying aircraft from factory or maintenance to airfield so the RAF could then fly the planes into combat.

Letters had been sent out to about 1000 male pilots asking if they were interested in joining the ATA. After interviews and flight tests, 30 civilian men were chosen to fly for the ATA, qualified pilots who did not fit RAF eligibility criteria. Initially, the first group of male ATA pilots were seconded to work out of RAF ferry pools. It might have seemed obvious that any female ferry pilots recruited by the ATA could simply join them. But the RAF was not keen on the idea of women pilots, civilian or otherwise, at that point: war might have just broken out and all resources were needed. But women pilots? It didn't seem likely.

If Gerard d'Erlanger was the driving force in the formation of the Civil Air Guard and the creation of the ATA, the individual who was largely responsible for the successful push to recruit women ferry pilots was the daughter of a well known Tory MP, Pauline Gower (see Appendix IV).

An experienced commercial pilot and a canny strategist, Gower had already made it known to the authorities that a women's section of experienced flyers could be deployed as delivery pilots, to complement the group of early male ATA pilots.

The combined efforts of these two people in the history of the ATA's female pilots cannot be underestimated. Certainly, both were well placed to influence events and put their case forward at the highest level (d'Erlanger was a member of a renowned banking family as well as an accomplished pilot). But most importantly, they were far-sighted enough to see that gender issues would be irrelevant at a time of national crisis: what mattered was that those civilians who were qualified to do the job as pilots were given the opportunity to do it.

On 23 September 1939, the Director of Civil Aviation Finance wrote to Gerard d' Erlanger giving him authority to form a small women's section of ATA qualified pilots. It would be separate from the men's section. Pauline Gower would be in charge of it. Qualifications for women pilots would be exactly the same as those for men. In theory, at least, women pilots could be employed in the ATA.

But the plan to recruit women stalled in those early months of the 'phony war' mainly owing to the resistance of the RAF. It was politely suggested that perhaps the women pilots could take other war jobs? They could be useful. But no, they couldn't fly with the Air Transport Auxiliary.

Yet events were moving fast. By November of that year, the picture was changing. It became apparent to the authorities that the ATA civilian flyer, either sex, had a key role to play. And Pauline Gower got her breakthrough agreement – an all women pool of women flyers could now be recruited to ferry small Tiger Moth training biplanes from the De Havilland factory at Hatfield, in Hertfordshire. Eight women pilots could be employed. More might be required by 1940.

Pauline Gower immediately got to work in December 1939. At 29, she was the newly appointed head of the women's section of the ATA. She had held a commercial pilot's licence for nine years, run her own aviation business and had completed over 2000 hours of flying time. Though in some instances, the experienced women pilots she was recruiting were older than her.

From her list of qualified women pilots, she invited a group of twelve to be flight tested at Whitchurch, near Bristol, on 16 December, taking them all out to lunch in Bristol before the test. Not everyone could be invited to join, so it was agreed that a few of the women would remain in their jobs. For the time being, at least.

The First Eight

Four months after war had been declared, eight women pilots joined the ATA on 1 January 1940. They were taken on as 2nd Officers. Their pay was set at £230 per annum, plus £8 a month flying pay (this was £80 per annum less than the earnings of a man on the same grade). The ATA male pilots were getting some assistance with their billeting (accommodation) expenses. Yet this did not apply to the women because they would be based at the Hatfield aerodrome to the north of London. They would be paying for their accommodation out of their own pocket. It definitely was nothing like equality. But thanks to Pauline Gower's determined lobbying, the equal pay issue would eventually be remedied in 1943, the first instance in UK history of equal pay for equal work.

The 'First Eight' were Winifred Crossley, The Hon. Mrs Margaret Fairweather, Rosemary Rees, Marion Wilberforce, Margaret Cunnison, Gabrielle Patterson, Mona Friedlander and Joan Hughes. They were all qualified flying instructors with impressive experience in the air.

Winifred Crossley, a doctor's daughter, had worked as a stunt pilot in an air circus. The Hon. Mrs Margaret Fairweather, had already worked as an instructor for the Civil Air Guard at Renfrew (her pilot husband Douglas had also signed up with the ATA). Mona Friedlander was, remarkably enough, an ice hockey international. Gabrielle Patterson, married with a young son, was the first woman in the country to work as a flying instructor; she had also been chief instructor and head of the women's corps at the Civil Air Guard in Romford, Essex. Joan Hughes had started flying lessons at fifteen and became the country's youngest girl flyer two years later. Rosemary Rees had completed a considerable amount of air touring. Marion Wilberforce was a pilot with her own Gypsy Moth. Margaret Cunnison was a flight instructor.

Out of this first group of pilots, Winifred Crossley, Joan Hughes, Marion Wilberforce, Rosemary Rees and Margot Gore (who would join the ATA a few months later and leave as a Commander) went on to complete nearly six years continuous ferrying for the ATA and remained with the organisation until it closed down when war ended.

The early women ATA pilots were mostly from wealthy backgrounds. But it is wrong to portray them as dilettantes, adrenalin junkies flying for kicks. Certainly, they had taken up flying pre- war because they or their families had the means to pay for lessons or even buy an aircraft – but they also flew because it was a hugely attractive proposition for the more adventurous, forward thinking type of 1930s woman: status alone did not satisfy their need for a challenge or excitement.

Much has been made, over time, of their social status, their depiction in glossy magazines, their upper crust partying in London hotels and nightclubs, their 'It' girl lives, in complete contrast to most of the country, struggling to cope with bombings, shortages, blackouts and wartime uncertainty. Certainly, in a superficial way, some of these upper crust flyers did bring a touch of much needed colour to the grim, grey perspective of war.

Diana Barnato Walker, millionaire's daughter and debutante, who joined the ATA in 1941, is a good example of this type of fast living wealthy ATA flyer (see Appendix IV). But the upper crust or wealthy women were as committed and determined in their desire to 'do their bit' for their country as anyone else; as they would prove over time.

Yet the dawn of those early days in 1940 at Hatfield aerodrome could hardly be described as glamorous. The eight women all lived in billets in the Hatfield area and worked out of a small wooden hut on the airfield. It was a cold and muddy winter. There wasn't much glamour in flying small, slow, training aircraft in freezing British weather in an open cockpit. Yet in this winter period they ferried over 2000 planes without any accidents. When you consider that many of the Tiger Moths being ferried from Hatfield were scheduled for storage in places like Kinloss and Lossiemouth in Scotland, ferry flights in those early years could also be an exhausting proposition.

The Hatfield pool could use three-seater Fox Moths to 'taxi' the pilots back from their short delivery trips to places like Kemble, in the Cotswolds or Lyneham in Wiltshire. But the only way back from a Scottish delivery flight was to take the night train south, often without a sleeping berth. Ferry pilots did not know where they would be flying to until the day itself, therefore there was virtually no chance of booking a sleeper. So the return trip from Scotland was often spent sitting upright in a crowded train that slowly crept its way south, through snowstorms and air raid alarms, often arriving in London many hours later than scheduled. Then, the woman pilot, laden down with her flying kit, would have to catch yet another slow train back to Hatfield, on occasion to report back to the ferry pool and discover she would be flying another plane up to the north of England.

The general public, of course, were completely unaware of what went on behind the scenes, although the opening of the Hatfield women's pool had been accompanied by a blast of publicity. The war had only just started and the need to create a positive perspective on Britain's air effort was important. So the 'First Eight' were photographed in flying gear and smart navy uniforms to be depicted in newspapers, newsreels and magazines everywhere. Pauline Gower was interviewed on the radio.

It certainly looked exciting and daring, this elite female group photographed scrambling to their Tiger Moths in their flying suits and fur lined leather flying boots. The image of goggles, flying helmet and sheepskin-lined Irvin jackets is instantly associated with the ATA female flyers but in fact, the jackets and leather boots were only ever issued to the First Eight and the goggles and helmet were required for open cockpit flying only.

The idea of bold women pilots doing war work usually seen as 'a man's job' did not please everyone. Equality was still a long way off. 'I am absolutely disgusted,' one reader wrote to *Aeroplane* magazine. 'When will the RAF realise that all the good work they are doing is being spoiled by this contemptible lot of women?'

Nor, alas, did the criticism come only from men. One letter, from a Betty Spurling, opined: 'I think the whole affair of engaging women pilots to fly aeroplanes when there are so many men fully qualified to do the work is disgusting! The women ... are only doing it more or less as a hobby and should be ashamed of themselves!' One wonders what the comments were at the Hatfield aerodrome when the women learned they had stirred up so much controversy simply by wanting to fly and help the war effort.

By July 1940, the Battle of Britain was about to start: Britain was about to engage in the fight for her life, a fight conducted in the air. The women ferry pilots had toughed it out through the winter of 1940. They had proven their worth. So it was decided that the women's pool at Hatfield should be expanded.

The First Year's Expansion
In the summer of 1940, two more experienced women pilots joined the pool and one of them was a flyer known to millions: Amy Johnson, or Amy Mollison, her name as a divorcée.

Despite her world-wide fame and fabulous exploits, Amy Johnson came into the ATA like the rest of the women. She took her ATA flying test in a Tiger Moth. Tragically, she only would fly for the ATA for a matter of months (see Appendix III).

In June and July 1940 the intake of women pilots was increased. Ten more women were recruited, bringing the female contingent up to 20. Now they would be allowed to ferry all types of non-operational trainer aircraft, rather than just the Tiger Moths, so they could be ferrying the full output of the Hatfield de Havilland factory where the Tigers, Oxfords and Dominies were produced, as well as the Magisters and Masters then being produced at Woodley, near Reading, Berkshire, at Phillips and Powis (later known as Miles Aircraft). Further training on the twin-engined machines was given throughout that summer. The workload was on the increase.

Those early ATA days saw meagre ground resources: the women pilots would have to take it in turns to act as Operations Officer, collecting all the necessary information about the location of balloon barrages, prohibited areas of flying, weather reports from the nearest RAF Meteorological Office, all the crucial information the ferry pilots needed to fly safely.

At one stage, before a standard operations book was established, Pauline Gower would have to take down over the phone details of the planes to be ferried, scribbling them on a slip of paper. It was all very piecemeal. Yet the method of allocating jobs and attention to detail was meticulous, as it would remain throughout the war.

By the end of 1940, the ATA had expanded. Eight ferry pools were in operation all over the country; this would double by the end of the war. Central Ferry Control at Andover, Hants, was the hub of all ferrying operations, allocating all the work daily to each individual ferry pool.

At that point, the ATA employed 616 staff. 243 were ferry pilots and over 10 per cent of these were female: the number of women ferry pilots had now increased to 26.

Amongst the latest intake were Lettice Curtis, whose five years in ATA led to her delivering nearly 400 four-engined aircraft,

150 Mosquitos and flying over 50 different types of planes (see Appendix IV) and Margot Gore, who would later be Commanding Officer of the second all-women ferry pool at Hamble, near Southampton.

The Ferry Pilots Notes

Few civilian pilots joined ATA in the early days with any serious technical knowledge or experience of military aircraft. 'A ferry pilot has so much to learn and remember that it is important that he is not taught one unnecessary fact.' This was the sound philosophy around which ATA training revolved. As aircraft production increased as the war intensified, however, it became clear that ATA pilots were likely to be flying a variety of aircraft types. So handling notes were devised. First issued in 1941, the notes ensured that pilots had all the information and data they required to fly a particular type of plane.

Two types of handling notes were designed: White notes (with a white cover) contained information on one type of plane only, designed for pilots to read when flying a particular type of plane for the first time. They also drew attention to any unusual features of a plane – a tendency to swing on landing for example.

The other type were the pocket sized Ferry Pilots Notes which contained information on all types of planes, produced in such a way that in theory, all the information the pilot needed was printed on one or both sides of a 6in x 4in card. In time, these notes became so important that no one would dream of flying without them. Their postcard type size meant they could simply be slipped into a pocket.

Producing these notes took a great deal of diligent work by the ATA's technical department. And while it may seem remarkable now to learn that wartime ferry pilots would sometimes be using what was, essentially, a simple printed primer to fly a brand new plane they had never flown before, this was war and time was at a premium. Training was given on each different group or class of plane. Yet so many different types of plane were being produced, the Pilots Notes were the most efficient way of ensuring the pilot had all the necessary information to do the job safely. By the time the war ended, there were cards with notes issued for over 70 different types of aircraft.

In 1940 plans were made to organise flying training into groupings of different types of planes. There were six main classes or groups of aircraft:

Class 1   light single-engined
Class 2   advanced single-engined
Class 3   light twin-engined
Class 4   advanced twin-engined
Class 5   four-engined
Class 6   sea planes

The general idea was that pilots joining ATA would be able to graduate through each class in turn, returning to training after time spent ferrying planes for conversion to the next class (organised training for Classes 4 and 5 did not start until 1943).

Ferry pilots did not always deliver the planes solo. In the case of the four-engined planes and a few of the 'twins', the ATA specified that a second crew member should be carried. In some cases this might be an assistant, an Air Training Corps cadet, or a flight engineer might be required as crew. At its peak, ATA employed 109 engineers – four of these were women.

The Spitfire Breakthrough

Through 1941, more female pilots were recruited. At Hatfield, a small flying school was established with female instructors. There were times when the main flying school at White Waltham HQ, near Maidenhead, Berkshire, was too busy to train male pilots. So a few men found themselves being taught by women.

In the summer of 1941, another significant landmark was reached: women pilots were authorised to fly operational aircraft. The oft repeated story about how this came about is that Gerard d'Erlanger and Pauline Gower were at a party when d'Erlanger said: 'I suppose there isn't really any reason why women should not fly Hurricanes.' The opportunistic Pauline replied: 'Fine. When can they start?'

In July 1941, four of the First Eight, Winifred Crossley, Margaret Fairweather, Rosemary Rees and Joan Hughes each climbed into the cockpit of a Hurricane and completed one circuit of the Hatfield aerodrome, watched by an admiring group of onlookers.

Just under two years into the war, the women had reached the point where they were able to share the workload of the male ferry pilots fully. That night, the four women celebrated, using their carefully hoarded petrol ration to drive up to London to dine at L'Ecu de France, a well known French restaurant in Piccadilly. In another two years time they would be tasked with flying all kinds of operational planes, including the heavy bombers.

The following month, Pauline Gower told attendees at a 'Women with Wings' fund raising luncheon that the prevailing theory concerning the women ferry pilots was 'the hand that rocked the cradle wrecked the crate'. Yet as she pointed out, the women ferry pilots had not broken the 1000 plus Tiger Moths they'd been required to ferry. Now, in principle, she told the guests, there was no limitation on the types of planes the women could fly. Not long afterwards, the ATA women pilots were being handed chits to ferry Spitfires. And they all loved flying them. As Lettice Curtis said of the Spitfire in her book, *The Forgotten Pilots*:

I never heard of anyone who did not enjoy flying it. It had a personality uniquely its own ... The cockpit of any single-seater aircraft is a very snug and private world. But to sit in the cockpit of a Spit, barely wider than one's shoulders ... was a poetry of its own.

Hamble and Cosford

As the war grew in intensity, recruitment of ATA pilots continued to increase and by the end of the summer of 1941 the number of women ferry pilots had reached 50. As production and deliveries were stepped up, the number of ATA ferry pools had also increased to twelve – eventually there were sixteen by the time the war ended.

At the end of September 1941, seven women from the women's ferry pool moved to Hamble, near Southampton, closer to the all important Vickers Supermarine factory at Southampton (which was producing the Spitfires) and other factories. Work at Hamble would involve shorter ferry trips of 20 or 30 minutes, enabling more aircraft to be ferried each day.

Wartime Spitfire production was based in two main areas, Southampton and Birmingham at Castle Bromwich. As a result, Hamble became the all-women's ferry pool to the south and Cosford on the Shropshire/Staffordshire border the all-women's pool in the Birmingham/Midlands area; though women could be posted, if necessary, to other pools at White Waltham, Prestwick, Ratcliffe, near Leicester and Kirkbridge, near Carlisle. The working routine was rigorous: thirteen days on, followed by two days off.

1941/2 was a cold, harsh winter and while runways were being constructed at many large airfields, the snowy conditions could sometimes make it extremely difficult to land the Spitfires. Yet no major accidents took place at this time. Hamble would remain a 'front line' aerodrome until war's end and it was attacked from time to time by stray enemy planes. It was a dangerous environment.

Nearly all the women interviewed for this book worked out of the all-women's pool at Hamble with elementary flight training carried out at Thame in Oxfordshire and Barton-in-the-Clay, Bedfordshire. Advanced flying training was carried out at White Waltham. (The only exception interviewed, Yvonne MacDonald, worked out of Cosford, the Midlands all-women's pool.)

Everyone recalls the camaraderie amongst the women and the well run efficiency of the ferry pool operation. The description by Diana Barnato Walker of the Hamble restroom in the morning, while the women waited for the weather to clear so flying could start, gives a vivid impression of exactly how it was. Her thoughts were recorded in E. C. Cheeseman's book, *Brief Glory*:

A jumble of chairs and tables and a few well arranged flowers first meet the eye, which scans to see 'Jackie' from South Africa turning her morning somersaults at the far end of the room. A radio (won by us for ten shillings in a raffle) provides the background to a cacophony of voices and other sounds until one sees next, as a contrast, an intent bridge four in session in a corner.

In the midst of these ... can be seen the more domesticated type cutting out a frock on hands and knees, with the material stretched beneath her on the rather uneven linoleum floor ... a backgammon game is going on and Maureen is trying to do a jig-saw puzzle in the small space left between the letter writers and the players ...

There is the eternal good natured bickering as to whether certain windows shall be open or shut. Jackie and her somersaults want them open; the backgammonites want them shut and so does Rose – except when she and Phillipa are doing their exercises ...

Suddenly the loudspeaker blares: 'Will all pilots report to the Operations Room for their chits!'

Everyone immediately drops what she happens to be doing and goes to the hatchway to be briefed for her job for the day. Then follows a scurry into lockers for maps and helmets, followed by a visit to the 'Met' for the weather and to the Maps and Signals Office for the latest information as to stray balloons and airfield serviceability. If a pilot gets a type of aircraft she has not flown before she goes to the library for a book of Handling Notes which will tell her all she requires to know about how to fly the machine. The taxi pilots study their carefully worked out itineraries and go out to the Anson or Fairchild to get the engines started and warmed up.

The day's work has begun, as the pilots plod out one by one across the grass, lugging parachute and overnight bag, none knows what the day may bring or whether she will manage to get back to base in time (or at all) for that long standing date for a lobster dinner at the Bugle Inn on the edge of the Hamble River.

The Foreign Legion of the Air

In December 1941, Japanese planes bombed Pearl Harbor and the Americans entered the war. The ATA would, over time, employ pilots from 25 different countries. The American pilots – 176 men and 27 women – made up the largest group from overseas.

The first five of the American women pilots to join ATA arrived in April 1942, under the leadership of Jackie Cochrane, an experienced flyer who had already set about organising a scheme for 25 American female pilots to join the ATA even before America had entered the war.

Jackie and her industrialist husband Floyd Odlum were extremely wealthy and influential, members of the US elite. And as head of the American 'gals' Jackie was an unpaid Flight Captain – though she did little ATA flying. Like the First Eight, she too became a glamorous character, based at the Savoy hotel in London, clad in expensive furs, turning up at White Waltham in a Rolls-Royce.

The contribution made by the American women to ATA was considerable: pilots such as Ann Wood Kelly, Virginia Farr, Edith Stearns, Jane Plant and Grace Stevenson completed nearly four years continuous ferrying, flying all types of aircraft, right up to heavy twin-engined bombers.

Other women from all over the world had joined them: from Canada, Australia, New Zealand, South Africa and others from closer to home, women from Ireland and Holland. The Poles included Stefania or 'Barbara' Wojtulanis (Poland's first female parachutist). Anna Leska (daughter of an army colonel who had already been flying unarmed for the Polish Air Force) and Jadwiga Pilsudska, daughter of Poland's Marshal Pilsudska. Anna and Jadwiga had been shot at in their escape from Poland by air.

Margot Duhalde (eventually known affectionately as 'Chile') came to England from Chile at age nineteen in 1941. She could speak no English at all – yet went on to rise to the rank of 1st Officer, continuing to fly with the ATA until the end of 1945.

Maureen Dunlop arrived from Argentina by ship in 1942. Of Australian and English parentage, she had obtained her pilot's licence at seventeen. A highly accomplished pilot, 1st Officer Maureen Dunlop became, thanks to that glamorous *Picture Post* photograph in 1944, the cover girl who unwittingly created the idea that the ATA was an all-female flying enterprise (see Appendix IV).

Starting from Scratch
By the spring of 1943, aircraft production was increasing and more ferry pilots were urgently needed. As mentioned earlier, the ATA even took the step of advertising (in *Aeroplane* magazine) for suitable trainee pilots without any flying experience at all. Men ages 28–50 and women ages 22–45 were invited to apply, provided they were over minimum height requirement (5ft 6in) were in good physical health and had an aptitude for sport.

No less than 2000 applicants wrote in offering their services. Such was the rigorous selection process, of these only seventeen applicants were eventually accepted for training as ferry pilots. Training itself was an expensive and time-consuming process. It is a measure of the high standards of the recruitment/interview process that such a relatively small number of pilots were eventually recruited this way.

By the autumn of 1944, aircraft production had peaked and the urgency about aircraft deliveries was gradually starting to diminish.

The number of women ferry pilots was now over 100, about 20 recruited in 1944.

Prior to the Normandy landings in the summer of 1944, certain ferry pools increased their pilot strength and some pilots volunteered for overseas ferrying into Europe. As the Allies advanced into Europe, male ATA pilots were ferrying into Europe by September 1944. But not the women.

Disappointed at the snub, Diana Barnato Walker later wrote: 'For many years the women pilots had been flying – and dying – in the same aircraft types and in the same conditions as the men, yet now we were being denied these foreign trips.'

Not for long. In the summer of 1944, Diana had married Wing Commander Derek Walker, newly appointed personal assistant to Air Marshal Sir Arthur Coningham. Derek, on a mission to deliver two Spitfires to Brussels, which had just been liberated, suggested to his new wife that she pilot one. Technically, it was breaking the rules. But she was off duty, on honeymoon. So in October 1944, the newlyweds piloted the two Spits to Belgium. It was an eventful mission, especially on the return trip when Diana got lost in fog. Her rule-breaking exploit made the point: women were capable of flying into Europe – though she was docked three months' pay for her reckless behaviour. By January 1945, ATA women pilots were officially given clearance to ferry into Europe: one of the earliest was 1st Officer Diana Ramsey, who had joined the ATA in 1941.

As the five women interviewed for this book remember so clearly, by spring, as the war was ending, the ATA too was gradually starting to wind down. Before the war in Europe had ended, all flying training had stopped. By summer 1945, one by one, the ferry pools were starting to close down. The horror of war was over; but putting it all behind them and stepping back into peacetime was a strange transition for many ATA women flyers.

For those hoping to keep flying, prospects were thin on the ground: with so many pilots leaving the RAF, they knew they would be very far down the line in the queue for jobs in aviation.

On 29 September 1945 at White Waltham, ATA made a very public farewell on a beautiful cloudless sunny day. After years of wartime secrecy around their work, thousands of people could now pay to be admitted to the airfield to inspect the aircraft and watch a flying display (the farewell Pageant was a fund raiser for the ATA Benevolent Fund for the widows and children of those pilots who had lost their lives) and it was the first Minister of Aircraft Production, Lord Beaverbrook, who opened the event. His speech paid fitting tribute to what the ATA had achieved:

> Without the ATA the days and nights of the Battle of Britain would have been conducted under conditions quite different from the actual events. The ATA carried out the delivery of aircraft from the factories to the RAF, thus relieving countless numbers of RAF pilots for duty in the battle. Just as the Battle of Britain is the accomplishment and achievement of the RAF, likewise it can be declared that the ATA sustained and supported them in the battle. They were soldiers fighting in the struggle, just as completely as if they had been engaged on the battlefront.

By the end of autumn, Hamble and Cosford pools had wound up. On the last day of November, the few remaining women still flying at White Waltham cleared out their lockers, returned their uniforms (they could buy them if they wished) and said their final farewells. On 30 November 1945, the ATA flag was lowered for the last time.

As for the women who flew Spitfires, a small group did go on to find careers in aviation (see Appendix IV) but most returned to civilian life and gave up flying for good.

Their exploits were, after the event, mostly forgotten until recently; but it is doubtful if any of the women themselves would have ever forgotten those years in the skies, when all that mattered was being handed a small slip of paper telling them where they were going that day – and whether they would be flying a couple of Spitfires or a brand-new bomber they had never flown before. Atagirls indeed.

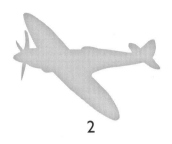

2

JOY LOFTHOUSE

Joy was born in Stratton, near Cirencester, Gloucestershire, on 14 February 1923. She joined the ATA on 28 December 1943, leaving on 30 September 1945 as a 3rd Officer. She flew 50 Spitfire deliveries and eighteen different types of planes.

They started life in a small English village in a working-class home in the Depression era. Yet the 'Gough Girls', Joyce (known as Joy) and Yvonne Gough proved to be an exceptional pair in many ways. They have the distinction of being the only two sisters to fly for the ATA. Plucky, sporty, competitive, bright young women from Cirencester, the 'Spitfire Sisters' as they've been called, had never even taken a joyride on a plane: for ordinary girls like these, piloting warplanes should have been an impossible dream.

Yet when the two girls, born fifteen months apart, learned that trainee pilots were being recruited *ab initio* they were eager to get involved. Of the 2000 applicants who applied to join the ATA in 1943 – when the urgent need for more ferry pilots meant advertisements for trainees without any flying experience – the Gough sisters were two of the seventeen who were finally accepted for ATA training.

They flew out of different Ferry Pools. Their lives took quite different paths after the war ended. Joy remained in the UK, following a brief period in Czechoslovakia, returning to her home town, Cirencester, much later on in life. Yvonne went to live in America and remained there. While sibling rivalry probably had something to do with them applying for the ATA at around the same time, 70 years on, their bond remained, irrespective of distance: two women sharing an irrepressible love of life, a poignant stock of memories of their war years and beyond; and that all important survivor's spirit – which served them so well throughout their lives.

Charming, exuberant and with a special, magnetic kind of energy that ignores the limitations of old age, their vivid recollection of those flying days remained undiminished.

'I Didn't Want the War to End'

We were a very basic working-class family. Most of our background was farming, agricultural. But I never felt we were poor while growing up. Perhaps children in country areas then were more fortunate: you had an allotment, you kept chickens, you could be much more self reliant than people in the urban areas.

My parents, Doris and Arthur Gough, had known harsh times. My father was in the First World War, in the Gloucesters for the last six months of the war. When he came out in 1919, he had no profession as such. I don't know what he did before we were born, I know he trained as a hairdresser. My mother's father, my grandfather, worked with horses on a farm.

My mum told me that once, when she was quite small, her father had scarlet fever, which was a bit of a disaster because he was the sole breadwinner. So my grandmother went to the farmer and asked could they have some wages in lieu?

I've never forgotten his answer. 'Oh you can always sell your piano, Mrs Herbert.'

So you really had to know how to stand on your own two feet then. Often, if someone lost their job or couldn't work through illness, that was it.

But children were allowed to be children then. They weren't mini adults like they are now. Growing up as young girls in Gloucestershire, I doubt if we ever left the area, except for a Sunday School outing. Yet our childhood couldn't have been better. It was wonderful.

My father came from a very athletic family and Yvonne and I inherited that. In the late 1920s, when we were small, he became a professional footballer, playing for Brighton & Hove. Yvonne and I always think that all those years helped us because we travelled around a bit as a family for a time and it gave us confidence we might never have had.

We'd stay in digs with a seaside landlady near Brighton. Or, when he played in the Midlands for a while, we all lived in two or three rented rooms. As a footballer, he could earn £5 a week – with a £2 bonus for an away game, which was good when you consider that the average agricultural wage was around £1 a week.

There we'd be, walking home hand in hand from school in our little green uniforms. On a Saturday, we'd often go to watch him play. Mother didn't work so she'd often go with him, watch him playing while a landlady looked after us when we got back from school. One day, Yvonne and I took the initiative and marched off to the Brighton and Hove football ground on our own and said: 'We don't have tickets but our dad's playing.'

We wouldn't have had that kind of confidence as children if we hadn't had that sort of childhood. And as sisters we were always very close, just eighteen months between us. We remained close all our lives. Right to the end, Yvonne would ring me every Sunday.

Unfortunately, my dad developed cartilage trouble so he couldn't play any more. At that point we came back to the Cirencester area, to Stratton. We didn't have a home to come back to after the footballing, so we all stayed with my grandmother for a while until we got our own rented home. My mother's family might have been quite poor but she and her elder brother played the piano and the organ at the local church. You've got to understand that what people would now call 'poor' was still a contented way of life. You didn't envy other people.

Living in a small village, the policeman, the schoolmaster, the vicar were all people to respect. If you didn't you'd get a clip on your ear. But there was no fear, living in the countryside. I was a tomboy, that would describe me best. I'd even fight Yvonne's battles for her sometimes. In the Brownies, I was always the one to climb highest – and I spent a lot of time in the swimming pool. I was so full of sport.

I wouldn't say we were exceptional. But we were bright. Yvonne passed her scholarship for Grammar School and then I did too, round about the time as our sister Wendy was born, ten years younger than us. I probably ignored her, poor little thing, I was so sport mad. There was only one scholarship a year from our village school out of about 50 or 60 children. The rest left at fourteen.

Our parents were very supportive of our education. Dad would have made far more of himself had he been educated, so he knew that learning was the answer to getting on in life. So when I got to Cirencester Grammar School to join Yvonne there, I was over the moon.

I can still remember the navy blue blazer and the gym slip which touched the floor when you knelt down. And the pale blue cotton dresses and the panama hats in summer, felt hats in winter. When I first went, you wore long black stockings to play hockey.

After a big classroom with village children, the new school was a revelation to me, A class for each year was a real novelty. My best subjects were English and, of course, sport. Netball, hockey, tennis, always playing to win. And swimming. By this time, 1934, my father was working as a supervisor at a local open air swimming pool in Cirencester and my mother ran the office there. The pool still exists, now it's run by a charity.

Much later, father had boys come back from Dunkirk, saying to him: 'Mr Gough, I'd never have come back if you hadn't taught me to swim, it helped us so much in the water.' But he was in and out of a lot of jobs in those years, it wasn't easy for our parents. Though my mother always helped bring in money. She was a wonderful seamstress and dressmaker, she made all our clothes, our tennis outfits, everything. Just before she died, I remember taking her to a Christmas party where almost everyone in the room came up to her and said: 'Do you remember, Mrs Gough, you made my wedding dress?'

I loved it so much, I probably spent too much time playing sport in those years from 1934 to 1939. School Certificate in those days meant passing eight subjects. Unless you passed your eight subjects you left at sixteen. I stayed on to take Higher School Certificate, taking additional maths. I intended to go into the Civil Service. Very few girls at my school got to university but I'd heard that in the Civil Service I might get the chance to travel. And they had wonderful sports facilities!

I'd only done one year of Higher School Certificate when war broke out. Yvonne left school early to start uncertificated teaching. And all the eighteen-year-old boys we knew were leaving, joining up. We thought war was exciting. Something different was going to happen. But then, we'd never experienced anything like it.

I thought it was a bit wimpish to stay at school. So I pestered my parents to let me leave too. Which was wrong. In the end, it was late in 1939 when I left school. I was supposed to go back the following September. But I didn't.

How could you forget the day the Second World War broke out? It was a warm summer Sunday and everyone knew Chamberlain was going to make some sort of announcement. Our father, of course, was very aware of what war really meant. He'd had six months in the trenches at the age of eighteen. He knew what it all meant. We sat round the radio, listening to those words you never quite forget: 'From 11.00am this morning, we are at war with Germany.'

Up to that point, we had led quite mundane lives, really. I hadn't travelled. I didn't really know what a German was. My parents, of course, were thankful there were no sons. At least their children wouldn't be getting involved. But they were very wrong.

I was sixteen and a half. I'd taken 'O' Levels the year before and I'd done one year of sixth form. So I went to work in a bank, the very same Lloyds bank that still stands on the corner in Cirencester town centre. The war changed everything very quickly. Three girls were taken on to work on the counter as cashiers within six months of war breaking out. That was something that had never happened before.

Of course, it was the phoney war in those first months. No planes came over to bomb Bristol, though this happened later on. The other two girls working with me on the Bank counter had boyfriends in the Navy and got married when they went off to war. In my mind, I thought I'd probably join up at eighteen.

Here in Cirencester, we're surrounded by airfields: South Cerney, Kemble, Little Rissington, Aston Down. So once the Air Ministry decided to get cracking on aviation, Cirencester was inundated with boys in RAF uniform. All my early boyfriends were in uniform. And, of course, as the war went on, the local boys were joined by uniformed lads from faraway places like Australia, New Zealand, boys you'd take home to your mum for tea. I met quite a few through serving them in the bank. And then there were the local hops and dances, the Young Farmers balls where you'd meet them and they'd ask you for a date.

A boyfriend in those days meant exactly that, even when I'd turned eighteen and had a proper boyfriend. It's not that we were so moral. It was more that unwanted pregnancy was strictly taboo, particularly in a rural area where everyone knew you. It was fear of illegitimacy that stopped you.

Despite the war, I was starting to be like a typical teenager, boyfriends in uniform, my clothes made by my mum, still playing tennis, still getting my mother to whip up a new dress in no time if I went to a ball. But the opportunity to do anything daring like flying was non existent. Even if you decided to join the WAAF, girls did not fly. But I wanted to keep up, know more about what the boys in uniform talked about. So I started reading a monthly magazine about aviation, *Aeroplane*. You couldn't just stand there, useless, dumb when the boys were talking about planes.

And so, in 1943, aged 20, I spotted the life changing advertisement in the *Aeroplane*. The ATA had run out of qualified original pilots, anyone with a fixed number of flying hours to their credit. The boys I knew often talked about what the flying instructors did, so I was already familiar with the terminology. The ad said they wanted people to be trained as pilots. You had to be over 5ft 6in, educated to at least 'O' Level and be willing to undergo a strict medical. And they were particularly interested in people with a good sporting background: they were looking for people with really good co-ordination skills.

Later on, people would say that the fact that both Yvonne and I both got in when all those other people had applied meant there was some sort of influence going on, which was complete rubbish. By the summer of 1943, Yvonne was a 21-year-old widow. She'd been married for just a year. Her husband, Tom, was a flying officer in the RAF. He'd been killed coming back from a raid on Germany. Yvonne had gone to live with his mother in Kent and was working in a factory. So while she too decided to apply, it was under her married name, from a different address. No one knew we were sisters. The only similarity on our CVs was the school where we'd been educated.

You have to remember that as young girls, the emphasis for us had always been on marriage and children. And marriage was for life, there were no life-long aspirations of work or careers for women. So being able to go into the Forces to be taught to fly was virtually undreamed of. Though from our parents' point of view, it wasn't seen as dangerous, rather something to be proud of, if you were chosen.

And, of course we were so young. Look at today's bungee jumpers. When you're young, you can do anything, you're full of confidence. And somehow, you have no responsibility: it's only you that gets hurt if anything bad happens. There's also the fact that everyone had to do something during the war.

Of course I could have stayed at the bank to the end of the war; my parents were far too old by then to be 'doing their bit'. But naturally, when Yvonne and I eventually came home in our ATA uniforms, they were very proud of us.

That ATA interview was very thorough. You were asked about school, what you'd been doing since war started, what you did for recreation. I think I interviewed quite well.

Another thing was, I'd spent my life being the younger sister. Yvonne passed the 11 plus first. She got into the sporting teams first, did her exams before me. Sometimes younger sisters go right under. But I had the kind of character that said: 'I'm going to do as well as Yvonne or die in the attempt.' That's how I was. And it worked out that we were both accepted around the same time. So at last, we were going to be doing something together. Sisterly equality.

But I couldn't just leave the bank. It wasn't that simple. You had to have a piece of paper from your employer to change occupation. And as a civilian trainee pilot, I wasn't going into the Forces. So my manager initially said no, I couldn't be released. It wasn't until December 1943 that he relented, so in the end I was three months 'behind' Yvonne. I was chasing her, as I'd been doing all my life. In those three months, when she'd tell me all about her adventures, I'd get quite resentful. But finally it was happening for me. I was going to fly.

By this time, I had a serious boyfriend. I'd met him when he came in to cash a cheque at the bank. George Hartman was a Spitfire pilot from Pilsen in the west of Czechoslovakia. And while I saw other people during my ATA years, he became, more or less, my permanent relationship. Though I'm sure he had other girlfriends too at the same time.

By December 1943 when I started, the ATA was very well organised. In the early days, the girls had really roughed it, but now the ATA had their own taxi aircraft to collect the ferry pilots from wherever they were. The taxi was a Fairchild Argus, which took three people plus the pilot. And they used an Avro Anson, which could take about 20 people – known as the 'workhorse' of the RAF. By this time the ATA had their own training establishment. Earlier on, ATA pilots were checked out by the RAF. So my training was at Thame, Oxfordshire.

The very first thing that hit you was nine days technical ground training at Thame. We learned how a plane worked, the internal combustion engine – quite new to me because I didn't drive a car – and, of course, a lot about the weather. They told us: 'England doesn't have a climate, it has WEATHER'. And we learned about navigation, which was map reading. At the end, there was a short exam. Only then, once you'd passed that hurdle, were you allowed to see a plane.

One day we boarded a bus and were driven for 45 minutes to a place called Barton-in-the-Clay, near Dunstable, Bedfordshire. (We quickly named it 'Barton in the Mud'.) And it was there that we saw our first plane, a single-engine low-wing monoplane, a Miles Magister. At last, our flight training had really begun.

It was a two-seater plane, one seat behind the other. The instructor talked to you through a Gosport tube, telling you exactly what to do. Oh, I was so, so anxious to do well in those first training days. The first few times, the instructor would say: 'You take the controls' and gradually you learned the basics, how to turn left, how to turn right, descend, then land: each one a memorable moment, though you knew you had to get it right. You couldn't be jumpy or nervous.

The instructors were all men, though about half the trainee pilots in my group were women. By this time, I'd made myself familiar with the history of the ATA; when the 'First Eight' had flown in 1940 it was the first time women had been allowed to fly service aircraft. As a fanatical cinemagoer, I'd seen it all on the Pathé newsreel. Yes, it was propaganda. We had to have that at the time. But I wouldn't really describe it as what they call PR nowadays.

The truly memorable first time, of course, is the first day they let you go solo after 10–12 hours' flying with your instructor, when the Commanding Officer of that group takes you up, and lets you do a solo circuit and landing. What a big moment it was when I climbed out of the plane to hear: 'Would you like to go to Thame tonight and tell your sister you soloed?'

I was nervous. Not for my own safety, more trepidation that I didn't do anything wrong. Everyone on solo day couldn't help but think: 'Will I make a mess of the landing?' But I didn't make a mess of it. That afternoon, I sat on the bus going back to Thame and our billet and could hardly contain my excitement. As soon as we got off, I rushed over to Yvonne to tell her the good news: I'd gone solo! She was already at a more advanced solo stage but still, it was terribly exciting for both of us.

I was full of it.

There was no mess at Thame, like the RAF. We were billeted in different houses in the area. I shared a room with a girl who didn't pass: she was upset but they gave her the opportunity to be a uniformed motor transport driver, so she spent the rest of the war at Kirkbride, in the Lake District, as a driver.

By this time in 1943, there was no daytime enemy activity. The Battle of Britain and the Blitz were behind us and any bombing took place at night. We didn't fly at night. Though this still didn't stop you from fearing for your friends or relatives, of course.

After your first solo, you moved on to more adventurous things, forced landings, how to get out of a spin. And then you did 24 cross-countries: you drew a line on the map allowing for wind direction, decided which compass point to put on. Some of these cross countries were with an instructor, some were solo. Again and again you were practising what you needed to know when you actually ferried aircraft across the country. It was very thorough training. People were killed – but no one was killed because they hadn't been taught properly.

The big excitement after completing the cross-countries was when you actually got your wings, the point where you were considered fully trained enough to get your uniform fitted. You had to be measured up for it at Austin Reed in London. Even the shirts were made to measure, even though you were still a cadet. The rank was cadet, 3rd Officer, 2nd Officer, 1st Officer, the same ranking British Airways used to use.

Of course, once Yvonne and I were in uniform, going home to see our parents was a chance for them to show us off to everyone. Sometimes people were unaware of what it all meant. 'Oh are you going as a driver?' people would ask. 'No. They're teaching me to fly,' I'd tell them, enjoying the look of sheer astonishment on their faces. Not many people knew about the ATA and what they did – unless you had some direct involvement with it.

After the cross countries you were sent on secondment to one of the ferry pools. The idea was to get you to know a different part of the country and also to get you used to the day-to-day running of a pool. There were two women-only pools, one in Hamble, and the other at Cosford, near Wolverhampton. I was sent initially to Cosford where I was only qualified to fly training aircraft, Class 1, Moths, Masters, Magisters.

The secondment was for six weeks. So in those weeks I did a lot of taxi work, picking up the more qualified pilots from wherever they'd taken a plane. It sounds like a long period of training. But there was a lot to learn; like the barrage balloons, on a chain 1000ft up in the air to protect all the ports and the factories. The balloons had been kept up from the early days of the war to deter low flying precision bombing. They could be wound up and down if necessary.

Obviously, they weren't going to let you move on to the next stage until you were ready. The big hazard, of course, was the weather. If the weather was bad, without radio, you never knew within a mile or so where you actually were. So you had to be completely confident that whatever you were being asked to do was within your capabilities. And our six months training was effectively slowed down by the weather. People who trained in the summer got through more quickly than those, like me, training through a winter. We had an 800ft ceiling – cloud had to be at least 800ft high – and 1500 yards visibility. But of course, you could take off and run into bad weather a few miles up the road.

Because we didn't live in a mess, like service people, you didn't see as much of other people. During the day, you were busy flying. You just went back to your own billet at night. So there wasn't as much communal life in the ATA except for the times when you were sitting around, waiting for the weather to clear.

But I still managed to see my boyfriend George, meet up with him in London when he was on leave. He was five years older than me and much more sophisticated and experienced. As a young girl who'd never encountered anyone from abroad, I was impressed with this rather charming man with his accented English, his impeccable manners and service training. And I'd also go home on leave frequently. We knew that while we were training in early 1945, the V1 and V2 rockets were about. But we'd still go up to

London on leave. We didn't care. And you have to remember that London hadn't experienced bombing for a couple of years before that time.

After secondment to the ferry pool, it was back to Thame to train on a more advanced plane, like a North American Harvard, a far more powerful machine and the first time I encountered a retractable undercarriage. All the training planes had had fixed undercarriages, it makes a big difference to the speed of the aircraft to have a retractable undercarriage.

You started out flying with an instructor on a Harvard, then solo, then you flew a few cross-countries in them. Just knowing you were whizzing through the air a little faster was so very exciting.

But the really big day, of course, was the day I went to the corner of the airfield and there was my first single-seater Spitfire. Oh, it was so powerful. After everything else you'd done before, this was like someone kicking you up the backside.

It was so light, compact, and incredibly easy to move. You almost had to breathe on the controls and they moved. So once I'd successfully flown the Spitfire, I was qualified to fly all Class 1 and 2 aircraft, including single-engine fighters. And I got my wider gold stripe as a 3rd Officer. At last I was going to do what I was employed to do: deliver planes.

Thankfully, I was posted south to Hamble. Though Yvonne remained at Cosford, which was a very different proposition for flying – all the smog and fog in the Midlands after flying in the Oxfordshire countryside. At Cosford, all the urban conurbations ran into each other, which made it harder to navigate. So I was delighted I got Hamble.

So by early summer, May 1944, I'd finished my training, won my stripe and started the work. It turned out to be a nice summer so there were times when I'd report to Hamble in the morning and fly straight away. You'd walk into the operations room, the hatch would open and the ops officer would hand out the chits.

A list of every aircraft that had to be moved came from HQ at White Waltham the day before and whatever had to be moved was allocated to each pool.

There were only two all-women ferry pools and the commanding officers of both pools were Margot Gore at Hamble and Marion Wilberforce, both very senior women. It was felt that it was right that they should be given command of a pool, but in those days, of course, they didn't like to put women in charge of men. Men then wouldn't take kindly to having a female commanding officer. So all the other pools apart from Hamble and Cosford had male Commanding Officers. That meant that Hamble really was an all-female setup, just one male engineer, that's all.

On a personal level, I was meeting women from very different backgrounds to my own, which didn't seem to make much difference. When I joined the ATA, I got teased about my Gloucester burr. And later, when I visited Mum and Dad in Cirencester, they'd say: 'Oh, you're talking posh now.' So I suppose I picked up a different accent simply because I was mixing with people who talked that way. I don't remember anyone in the ATA with a regional accent, though of course there were many people from other countries.

One of my best friends in the ATA, Jean McPherson, had been presented at Court before the war. So I was aware that most of the girls were from very moneyed families but I'd been very lucky: there were only about half a dozen training courses for people like Yvonne and I, those people taught to fly from scratch. At one stage, I went home with Jean to meet her family. They were obviously moneyed – they had a housekeeper, for instance – but I wasn't ashamed or self-conscious about my background. I was forever grateful for the education my sister and I had, which set us on the right track.

As for the flying, each day varied tremendously. You never got up in the morning knowing exactly whether you could get back to base or bad weather would stop you. Sometimes you'd be given a plane to transport from A to B. Sometimes we were taken to the factory at Eastleigh to collect a Spitfire. But mostly the planes we were transporting were from Southampton to the area around the Cotswolds or the South Coast. We would transport the planes to the maintenance unit where the radio and guns were fitted. But we were not trained to use these things: it would have involved much longer training to train us for radio. When you delivered and left the maintenance unit you were collected by taxi aircraft to take you to the next job.

I flew 50 Spitfires – nothing compared to what the other girls flew – but I did have my scary times. One day, I was given a chit to pick up a new Spitfire from the factory and I found myself in a fix right after take-off: I was heading towards some barrage balloons. The later versions of the Spitfire, the Marks 12–14, had much more powerful engines. Everyone thinks of the Spit with the old Merlin engine. But this was replaced with a Griffon engine later in the war. I'd been told by the senior girls what to look out for with the more powerful engine – 'This is a different beast altogether, Joy,' they warned me. 'Open up the throttle gently because it will have a pronounced swing on take-off. And you have to use the opposite rudder to straighten it out.'

Of course, I did everything they told me: opposite rudder to counteract the swing. But to my horror, the Spit was still heading towards the barrage balloons. It felt like minutes of sheer terror. But in fact, it was a matter of seconds. Because the minute the plane gets height, the controls come into play – and the controls keep it straight. So in reality, you straighten up quite quickly. But for that minute or two, my brain was racing: 'Am I going to hit that cable? Or whizz through it?'

But you're so busy doing what you think is the right thing, you don't actually panic. And that is where the training came into play. You had been trained to deal with it. And because of that training you have the confidence, the feeling, 'Well, they wouldn't put me in this position if I wasn't capable of dealing with this.'

There were other bad moments. We had casualties in ATA and I'd say 80 per cent were due to bad weather. Not many were pilot error, maybe 20 per cent. One fellow who trained just before me flew into the Wrekin (a hill in Shropshire). Without a radio or pinpoint accuracy you could be just a mile out and hit high ground when you didn't expect it.

You weren't always told about these fatal crashes. But we were such a small organisation, the grapevine always told you what had happened.

6 June 1944 was, of course, D-Day, the Normandy landings. We'd been delivering planes that spring in the run-up, upwards of 20 fighters a day, Typhoons, Tempests and Spitfires flown straight to the squadrons on the south coast airfields. For a few months beforehand no one had been allowed to travel to the south coast of England for pleasure; they knew people would see the preparations for D-Day. From the air, we could see all the mechanised vehicles stacked up in the lanes, you could have walked across to the Isle of Wight on the landing barges. The Germans had high reconnaissance aircraft. But they still thought we'd go the shortest, Pas de Calais route. No one dreamed we'd take the longer route into Normandy.

That morning, 6 June, if you took off from Hamble, the Solent was empty. The barges were gone. We knew it was the beginning of the end. We were discouraged from talking about what we saw from the air, of course. The tiniest little bit of information might seem insignificant. 'Be like dad, keep mum,' was the slogan. That sounds funny now, but too much was at stake then.

Sometimes, because of the weather, you'd spend days 'stuck out' before you could be cleared to fly. On one occasion I was flying a single-engine Barracuda of the Fleet Air Arm. I flew it from Hamble, right over the Cotswolds – where the ground is higher so you could fly under the cloud. I landed at Moreton-in-Marsh and the weather didn't clear for three days. So I managed to hitchhike back to Cirencester to see my parents. In those days, hitching was safe. Especially if you were in uniform.

You'd work twelve or thirteen days, then get leave. I'd sometimes go to see George, where he was stationed in Kent. He flew in the Czech Spitfire Squadron No. 310 for the RAF Fighter Command.

When I visited him at the station there'd be parties. Or if we met in London we'd dance at nightclubs, places like the Embassy Club, the Astor, The Mirabelle, dancing on tiny dance floors. And dancing, of course, was important then because it was probably the closest you got to a man. And I was in the officer class world, quite different from the Hammersmith Palais, where the Americans went and did the jitterbug. I definitely wasn't a jitterbugger.

If it could be arranged, sometimes you could get a job flying into where you wanted to be just before your leave. Once, I was going on leave and given a Spitfire to fly into Aston Down, near Stroud, not far from home. A single-seater plane has a bucket seat, so the parachute was my seat (you needed your parachute if you were flying single-seater flyers).

I knew I'd be hitchhiking and I didn't want to hitch with a parachute and have to carry it around on leave. So I left it behind and flew the Spit sitting on my bag. Of course, the aircraft engineer was appalled.

'No parachute, mam?'

'We don't fly high enough for a parachute,' was my response.

As a 3rd Officer, I earned £9 a week. At the bank, I'd earned £1 10s, when my first ever week's wages went on buying a pair of high heels. I don't recall saving much. You paid your own train fares. And you paid for your own living out, what you did when you went to London. Though apart from that there wasn't much to spend money on: the rationing and the clothing coupons restricted your spending. All you could spend on a meal out was 5s.

Of course, some people got round it but in an average place, like Lyons Corner House, that was all you could spend.

In February 1945, I went back to White Waltham for more training. Now I could fly the Class 3, Oxford, the Anson and the Rapide, light transport planes with twin engines (known as 'light twins'). But within a few months, of course, it was starting to end. By the time of VE Day, 8 May, a lot of the ATA pools were already closing down. A lot of the men were only too glad to leave. But in all honesty, I never wanted to leave.

So when Hamble shut down, they sent me to Sherburn in Elmet, near Leeds, where we were flying a lot of Fleet Air Arm planes up to Scotland. It should be remembered that before VJ Day in August 1945, no one knew about the atomic bomb. The Americans were still fighting their way across the Pacific, everyone thought we'd have to invade Japan. The Fleet Air Arm aircraft were due to go onto the aircraft carriers to continue the war against the Japanese in the Far East. We were only told what we needed to know.

It's incredible to think of now but news was very tightly controlled. As far as I was concerned, war continued in another part of the world.

So when we heard about this colossal bomb dropped on Japan, we couldn't even comprehend what sort of bomb it was. What was a hydrogen bomb? I was there, in the thick of it, alongside other service people. But we didn't know a thing about this huge secret. Right up to the last minute, before Hiroshima, we were doing the normal wartime things, thinking the Japanese war might go on for a long time: we all knew they'd have fought to the last man. And we, in turn, would have lost millions of lives.

Even after VJ Day, we were still moving the Barracudas and Seafires (adapted to land on aircraft carriers) up to Scotland. There were fields upon fields in Scotland with aircraft with their wings folded up – which were eventually destroyed and used for scrap.

I flew my last flight for the ATA in September 1945. For me, it was devastating. The excitement of this amazing wartime job had gone. No civilian job could possibly live up to it. I certainly didn't intend to go back to the bank.

To be perfectly honest, I wanted the war to go on as long as possible: wartime gave many women something they'd never had: independence, earning your own money, being your own person. Once you married, everything changed dramatically. And I had no aspirations to continue flying, the men were pouring out of Bomber Command into any commercial flying job available. It wasn't until the 1950s that Dan Air had the first women on the flight deck as pilots or co-pilots. So commercial flying came too late for most of the more senior girls in ATA.

By now, George and I were officially engaged. He'd gone back to Czechoslovakia in August; he couldn't wait to get back to his own country. There was no thought of him staying here at that time. He'd fought in the French air force until Dunkirk. Then he'd come to England. The plan was, I'd fly to Prague and we'd get married in the New Year.

In November, White Waltham HQ held a big ATA get together. Everyone got up and said all these nice things about us. But by the end of 1945, the ATA shut down completely.

I loafed around at home until Christmas. Then, as planned, I flew to Prague on 31 December. It was bad weather. I flew off in an old Junkers plane that looked like it was made of corrugated iron. It was flying back repatriating Czech civilians. And there were English girls, like me, who were also marrying Czech pilots. It was a long journey, we wound up staying overnight in Brussels en route.

If you ask me what I was thinking then, I'd say: 'Well, this is a bit more exciting than living in a little village in Gloucestershire.' Looking back, I was so young when I met George, had I been a bit older, things might have been different. But women then accepted that marriage was the ultimate step: our world was so different. I'd had a very exciting, glamorous wartime job. And the fuss that was made about us as a group of women pilots was sometimes embarrassing. But I was just the same as all the women who stood at assembly lines, putting screws in or carried stretchers, drove ambulances. Everyone did something in the war. But now it was over.

I arrived in Prague on New Year's Day, 1946. George was stationed there but he wasn't waiting for me at the airport: he was at home in Pilsen, 55 miles from Prague, but he had a friend there to greet me. Yet I found that living in Prague wasn't too difficult. A lot of people spoke English, it didn't feel too strange.

Air force people who had flown in the war got priority accommodation and we were offered a flat. Then we got married. We had a church wedding on 17 March 1946. I still wore my ATA uniform. George's mother would have liked a big white wedding but we'd managed to marry in church with a vicar who spoke English. Though he was obviously reading the same speech he'd used when the American Forces servicemen had been marrying local girls.

It sounded really odd. It went something like: 'You are taking this young lady far away from her home to a strange land.' Well, in my case, that was partly true. The plan was for us to remain in Czechoslovakia. And, of course, with a wartime romance, you didn't really know the person but you didn't think 'Oh, shall we try living together first?' I don't think it's a bad idea to grow into the idea of someone else. But then? A reasonably well brought up young girl just … got married.

Our flat was in the old part of Prague, in an old building. Then George was posted from Prague to Brno and we got another flat, a better one, that had been taken off the Germans. I can still remember the garage outside. Across the wall someone had scrawled in huge letters: *Rauchen Verboten* (Smoking Forbidden). Of course, at that point, they were confiscating a lot of things from the Germans; which the Germans, in turn, had confiscated from the Jews. We were allowed to go to huge depots to choose furniture and china for our flat, but it was all very spartan. And there was even less food around than in England; food rationing was very strict.

A year later, my eldest son Peter was born in Brno in January 1947. We had hoped that George would be able to travel to England once Peter was born. In fact, it was my mother who wound up seeing more of Czechoslovakia than I did because George showed her around a lot when she came to visit us and see the baby. As for me, with a new baby to look after, I blithely assumed that there'd be plenty of time to see the rest of the country. But it didn't work out that way.

By 1948, life in Czechoslovakia was getting dangerous. The Soviet occupying forces arriving in Prague were sometimes undisciplined, violent. They'd break into homes, go into buildings, wrench off the taps. So if George had to go away overnight, leaving me and Peter alone, he'd have to leave me a gun on the bedside table. And when the Czech Communist Party, backed by the Soviets, took over the Government in February that year, it became obvious: there was no future there for us.

Getting out was no easy matter. Week after week, I'd go to the Czech Embassy, my little boy in my arms, to get permission to come home. I couldn't tell my family I was coming back for good because I didn't know what was going to happen.

At first, they refused to give us exit visas. What was holding me up was the fact that I held a Czech passport. But fortunately for me, the British Government put their foot down – by then German girls were marrying British Occupation servicemen in Germany so my case was hardly exceptional – so Peter and I got out legally.

For George it was very different. Anyone who had fought alongside the Allies was under suspicion as far as the Communists were concerned. So George was put in jail, on a trumped up charge, for a while, mainly to show the authorities' disaffection with those who had fought in the war for a foreign power and taken English wives.

They let him out just before Peter and I left, fortunately. But when he waved us off at the airport, we still didn't know what would happen to him or if he'd be able to leave. I'd been back home living with my parents for several months before I got the news that George was in Austria. He was only allowed to return to England because he had a British wife and child.

When he got back, in May 1948, we remained with my parents for six months. We had no money at all. It seemed likely that he'd get back into the forces and finally in December they took him back into the Royal Air Force with a permanent commission and he became, eventually, a squadron leader.

So that was how I became a RAF wife for 20 years. I am pretty certain that our wartime experiences had an effect on us in civilian life. But then you didn't confide in people, talk about your feelings, the way people do now. I'm not particularly good when it comes to discussing feelings, emotions. But I can talk about what happened to us.

Once George got back into the Air Force we left my parents and moved to Odiham, near Reading where we lived in rented digs for a while. Then we moved into married officers' quarters on the base. Our second son, Michael, arrived in 1951.

It was a happy time when I was pregnant with Michael. In the RAF your social life was made for you, coffee mornings, cocktail parties, tennis, squash games on the base. It was all there. You didn't even have to go out to shop if you didn't want to, there was the NAAFI shop for us.

We wanted a family. I can remember going to the doctor before Michael because I was worried I wasn't getting pregnant quickly enough. I still played quite a lot of sport. I played for Basingstoke Ladies Hockey Team at weekends and we both played a lot of tennis. 'You'll never get pregnant, you're always rushing around the place,' George used to warn me. For him, it was an exciting time. He was in an operational squadron flying De Havilland Vampire jets at the time.

If there was a problem, it was the rationing. It continued after the war ended. You still had coupons, you couldn't get extra just because you were service. Of course, you could eat in the mess at night – if there were ladies' nights. But still, I was content with life, happy in my own skin, as they say, I don't reach out for the unattainable. Life was good.

Then we moved to Middle Wallop base in Hampshire. George was one of the first people to be in a helicopter squadron. By now, Peter was going to school. I can remember being there in 1952 for the Queen's Coronation, one bitterly cold day with the wind blowing across Salisbury Plain. At one point, I had to have an operation – a partial thyroidectomy – so my mother had to come and look after the two boys. Men weren't domesticated then, particularly George who was an only child and later always had a batman to clean his shoes and look after his uniform each day.

The postings were usually for two years. Because George had done a helicopter course, the next move was to Leuchars, near St Andrews in Scotland, where the helicopters were most useful as rescue aircraft if a boat got into trouble.

Our third child, Lyn, was born there in 1955. So I had one Czech, one English and one Scottish child with four years between each one. Living up there meant very basic accommodation. To begin with we lived in a Nissen hut. It was a bit cold and wild, living up there.

As a father, George was very good. He was strict, the children respected their father. And we were a family on the move all the time during the 1950s. For a while, we were stationed near Middlesborough and then near Scunthorpe. But of course, by this time George's RAF career as a squadron leader was coming to an end. He had a permanent commission. But unless you are earmarked for higher promotion, you don't know what the future holds. Of course, he could have stayed in the RAF until 55. But George chose to come out in his mid 40s. And that was when it all started to change.

By the time the 1960s dawned, our life was different. George had been a lifelong gambler, poker, betting on the horses. So he decided to put his RAF redundancy money into what he loved: he bought a share in a betting shop in Portsmouth. I admit, I was disappointed he didn't opt for something more settled. But we prospered, there was good money in it. The boys both went to Portsmouth Grammar – we paid for Peter and Michael got a scholarship – and I was very proud of them. By the time he was eleven, Peter had been to eight different primary schools, yet he still came out tops.

Financially, we were better off than we'd ever been. We even bought our own house just outside Portsmouth, the first time we'd ever had a settled home. Wonderful, especially when after years of two year stays in quarters, I always hated leaving a good garden.

George very much wanted to be his own boss and because the betting business was his livelihood, he loved going to race meetings. And that's where we differed. He was doing what he enjoyed. But I wasn't. I really missed our old life, the Air Force way of life, the people we socialised with. I had friends, other parents from the children's schools. But I missed the companionship of other Air Force wives. So by the late 1960s, the marriage wasn't going well at all.

We didn't fight. In a way, we were typical of many rushed wartime marriages or couples who married the minute war was over. The world had changed. And I started to think I should make my own decisions. I decided that if I was ever going to have independence again, earn my own living, I had to get on with it. So I enrolled at Teacher Training College in Portsmouth. As it ended up, my husband wished I'd never gone.

I'd signed up for a two-year mature applicants' course. And naturally, there were a lot of married people on the course, a lot of ex-service people all wanting to get a teaching certificate. And in the way of these things, I met someone on the course with whom I had a lot in common.

Charles Lofthouse was an ex-RAF bomber pilot. He'd survived 30 bombing raids during the war and had been awarded the OBE for rescuing five aircrew from a Stirling bomber that had crashed at Waterbeach airfield, in Cambridgeshire. The plane was 30ft above the ground when the trainee pilot mistook a shallow layer of fog for the runway and tried to land. The plane came down so heavily, the undercarriage collapsed and the punctured fuel tanks set the plane alight. Charles and two ground crewmen fought their way into the wreckage to drag five men out. Unfortunately, he'd been shot down over Berlin in 1943 and spent the last two years in Stalag Luft 3 (the scene of the Great Escape). But he stayed in the RAF after the war.

Just like me, he'd married as soon as war ended. And as it turned out, we both had rocky marriages. Teaching to me at that time was a way of having an independent life. Breaking up my marriage, even though things were bad, had not been on the agenda. But of course, when you meet someone else you realise that, perhaps even in your 40s, it might not be too late to make an entirely new life for yourself.

At the same time, I started to realise that George's skiing trips without us or his evening trips to the races – or the nights when he said he was playing cards into the wee small hours – weren't quite the truth. No one ever walks out on a really happy marriage. And it's never one person's fault. But I have to admit, had I not met Charles and formed a close relationship with him, I'd have probably stayed with George, if only for the sake of the children.

Charles' marriage wasn't going well either. So we were both looking at our lives, our children, our marriages and wondering: dare we try to start another life together? The divorce laws then were very different, much more difficult than they are today. There hadn't been any infidelity, so George couldn't sue me for infidelity. Technically, if I left our home, it would be desertion. But then he would have to ask for the court's discretion – because of his own adultery. Obviously, he could fight against that. It was messy. But I wasn't really interested in legal tit for tat. I just wanted out.

By the time my two-year course had ended, things were so unpleasant at home, I decided to leave my husband. The boys were away at University. Lyn was still at home. But I just left the house. Physically, I'm tough. But morally, on the emotional level perhaps I am a bit of a coward. I don't show much emotion.

At the time, Birmingham was seen as a city of opportunity. So I went up to Birmingham on my own and found a job in a residential school, where I could live on the premises. Lyn stayed at home with George. Yes, it was selfish but I'm happy to say it has never affected my relationship with her. Although it would be a long time before I saw her and she could come and visit me.

By this time, George knew about Charles and I. I think they may have met up at one stage, but I don't know for sure. I just wanted the divorce to happen without knowing about the details. For about a year, Charles and I would communicate through his sister in Weston Super Mare. Then, finally, he left home and got a job in Birmingham. His wife was a Catholic and they had four children, theirs too had been a wartime marriage, she was a war widow when they married.

So the whole thing was a huge wrench for everyone. Looking back, probably no one thought it would last. After all, I'd been married to George for 22 years. I suspect it hit my parents very hard: their thinking would have been 'put the children first'. As a result, there was a huge rift between me and my parents, we were not in touch for about a year. Yet when I contacted them again, after the divorce, they were delighted. They'd had time to get used to it.

Who knows how things might have been had I met Charles during the war? We might have hit it off right from the beginning. It took a long time for the divorce to come through. We didn't live together while we were waiting, only when we saw that it was finally due to happen. In the end, we took a flat together in Castle Bromwich for a few months, then the divorce came through. Not long after we had a registry office wedding.

After the divorce, I never had any contact with George. Yet there were no problems with the children. Peter was at Oxford – he'd won a scholarship. Michael was at university at Reading. And Lyn came to stay with us in our first flat in Birmingham. Charles had a daughter the same age so as time went on, we were friendly with his family – and his ex-wife. You can't let the children suffer.

I'd found the two years I spent working and living at the residential school quite hard, the hardest of my life. My living quarters consisted of a tiny room next to the junior dormitory and, through the night, I was in charge. The school was for delicate children, ages 7–16, children with asthma, spina bifida, sickle cell anaemia. So if a child woke up in the night with a severe asthma attack, I was the person who looked after them. Then you were up again to teach at 9 the following morning.

There were other staff to help but the work was demanding, both emotionally and physically, with weekend duty sometimes. I taught a junior class, but because I wasn't qualified to teach music, I taught all the games – which of course, I loved. But it was exhausting. But once Charles and I were married and settled, life was happy and settled again.

Eventually Charles got a job as a senior master at a primary school in Rye, Sussex and after a few months job hunting, I got a teaching job at a senior school in Rye. Because of my experience, I got a job as Head of their Remedial Department and taught English in the main school.

We didn't have a lot of money. But what we had in mind was to buy something old and do it up. We wound up buying an old village school in Icklesham, between Rye and Hastings. Charles was a great DIY man and he set about making a home for us out of the old school.

We were still teaching and eventually Charles won a headship of a small village school. I was so delighted for him. He was a war hero, yet had not got to the top in the RAF. But at least he had in teaching.

I was 60 and Charles not quite 65; he was adored by parents and children alike. But unfortunately there were union problems with staff striking. So retirement came a little sooner than we'd anticipated. Finally, because I'd always wanted to return to the Cotswolds, we came back to Cirencester and bought a house about a quarter of a mile from where I live now, opposite Deer Park School, where I did a bit of supply teaching.

Charles maintained his links with the past. He was secretary of the local RAF Association. Like a lot of people who survived the war, he still felt he owed something to those who hadn't. He worked hard at that. And he was also secretary of 7 Squadron, his wartime squadron, so we travelled frequently for RAF reunions all over the world, Canada, Australia, New Zealand, all over Europe. We did a lot of travelling, thank goodness, while we were both fit. And, of course, we'd go to see Yvonne in America frequently.

I loved the reunions. It was my kind of life. That shared wartime experience binds people together in a way people couldn't understand now. Our friends were mostly ex-Air Force people.

Charles and I were married for 30 years. By 2002, we knew that he had circulation and heart problems. We'd gone to see a specialist and were told he needed a stent fitted. That same weekend in July, I woke up and went downstairs. The fire was blazing away. And there was Charles, sound asleep in the chair in front of the fire.

I just went into the kitchen and got him a cup of tea, as usual. Only then, when I went to wake him, did I realise what had happened. No struggle: a peaceful death aged 80 in his own home, in front of the fire. Yes, it was a terrible shock. But we are only here once. And we had a great deal of happiness together, despite what had happened before. He is buried at the All Saints Churchyard at Longstanton, the spiritual home of RAF 7 Squadron.

George died in 2006 at the age of 88. He'd remarried and lived in Portsmouth. We never really kept in touch, only through our children.

My eldest, Peter, married while still at Oxford and worked for Roche as a biochemist; he's now retired. His son, Daniel, my only grandchild, now lives in Germany. Lyn married a widower with two grown-up children, she lives in Wiltshire. Sadly, my middle son, Michael, died in 2004, aged 53.

I did see George just once, at Michael's funeral. His sight was very bad then and we chatted about old times. There were no great feuds or family battles. Though there'd been no contact between me and George for all those years, there was no residual nastiness about the divorce. I'm not a confrontational person, anyway.

People often ask me, does it all seem real now, flying Spitfires while war and chaos was all around you? I always say that they were such impressionable years, they never quite leave you. I still see the surviving Spitfire Girls at reunions, though there's so few of us left now. Mary (Wilkins) Ellis is one I occasionally see from our flying days at Hamble. She ran a car, so she'd often give me lifts.

In a way, we were trailblazers for women's emancipation. It was the first time ever in this country that women achieved equal pay with men, thanks to the efforts of Pauline Gower, that was one consequence of us flying for the ATA. We weren't like the Pankhursts. But people will always be able to look back at us and say: 'Look what these women did during the War.' Freydis Sharland said it and I think it probably does apply to all the ATA women: 'They were the most important days of my life.' But when you really think about it, anyone would say that about what they did in wartime. Maybe people think we hark back on it too much. But for us, well, that *was* our life.

My philosophy through life has always been what is the good of being dissatisfied and thinking 'if only'. If you want to be happy, you have to be satisfied with the life you've made for yourself. It's no good envying others. You say: 'This is what I've chosen, it was my own choice.' And if I didn't make the right one? Well tough. Just get on with it.

Looking back, I took on something different, leaving a very safe bank job to go flying. Then I upped sticks for Czechoslovakia, then, later, I made a choice to leave my marriage. I've always felt in command of my life. To me, there's no point in going through life being unhappy when you only get one shot at it.

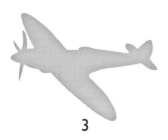

3

YVONNE MACDONALD

Yvonne Gough, Joy's older sister, was born in Stratton, near Cirencester, Gloucester, in 1921. She died on 14 September 2015, just five days before her 93rd birthday. She joined the ATA on 6 September 1943, leaving on 30 June 1945. She flew 53 Spitfire deliveries and eighteen different types of aircraft.

'It Was Like Having Wings Sewn on your Back'
One of my most vivid memories of our childhood in the countryside is when Joy and I, out playing one afternoon, found ourselves by the driveway of a very big, grand house when the owner of the house – let's call him the lord of the manor –came up the road on horseback. He'd been out hunting. To two little four- or five-year-olds, he made a huge impression in his red hunting gear. We'd never seen anything like this before.

Spotting us standing there, he said: 'Would you like something nice to eat, girls?' and handed us a carefully wrapped up package. Inside the package were wonderful sandwiches, with all the crusts removed. His housekeeper had obviously made them for his lunch. But rather than go back home with them uneaten and face her wrath, he thought he'd give them to us.

So we ran home with the sandwiches and gave them to mummy. We had a very happy childhood, though our father had an up and down working life: after the years playing professional football, things got quite tough especially through the Depression. Our father was out of work for ages in the 1930s. But that man on horseback was our first glimpse, if you like, of the big class divide that existed back then. Maybe he thought we were two hungry little waifs – which wasn't the case at all.

As sisters, with just a year and five months between us, we were always together. Joy was the beautiful child, blonde with dark eyebrows. When Joy was about four or five, mother sent a picture of her off to a beautiful baby contest. Of course, I was terribly hurt by this. It meant that I wasn't as attractive as my sister. And that idea stayed with me, even when I'd grown up. If I took a boyfriend home, I'd always be secretly afraid they'd like Joy better. But no one ever wanted to switch. Years later, of course, we'd just sit and giggle together about it all.

The one thing we both excelled at as we grew up was sport. We won everything. I was captain of everything: tennis, field hockey, netball, swimming. And Joy and I played to win. Eventually we were known locally as 'The Gough Girls' because of this.

We'd obviously inherited that athleticism from our father and though we didn't know it, our love of sport would eventually be a big factor in getting us into the ATA. Growing up in the Gloucestershire countryside, we weren't thinking about things like politics or war. When war broke out, we were teenage girls, just starting to work, go to dances, have boyfriends. It was all very innocent back then. But when the war came, it turned everything upside down.

In 1939, when war broke out, I'd planned to go to Teacher's College in Putney, London. But my father, who'd been through the First World War, was very nervous about that idea. Nobody knew what to expect; initially, we all thought the Germans were coming over to invade within a matter of days or weeks. So I started teaching at a primary school in Cirencester. To be honest, teaching scared the life out of me. I was just eighteen; I felt I hardly knew more than they did.

At that point I was going out with my first boyfriend, Peter Cumley, a boy I'd known at school. Cirencester started to be surrounded by aircraft bases, they were building them all over the south of England, so we were in the heart of things as we got older.

Peter signed up for the Royal Air Force the day after his eighteenth birthday. He was more of a good friend, I wasn't expecting to marry him. He was killed at nineteen. He went down over the English Channel during the Battle of Britain, September 1940. I've been to the memorials in England where his name is inscribed on the wall, along with all the other people killed then; we knew so many like him. Between us, there were about eight young men Joy and I had met in those early war years who didn't make it. We were all so unformed. And innocent.

But you don't just recall the sad things. I can still remember my very first evening dress, made for me by my mother. Despite the war, people still went out to dances sometimes, enjoyed themselves. Our parents loved dancing, we'd all go to a dance together on occasion. And it was still a relatively quiet country life. Most of the fighting was on the south coast. I can remember a plane that had been shot down not far from Cirencester, that was a big excitement. But we didn't get as much of the bombing as some other parts of the country.

Of course, the blackout played a big part in our lives. We had a neighbour on our street who complained endlessly because one of the boys that came to take Joy out had a white car. This neighbour kept asking my mother to do something about it; she was worried because the white car was sometimes parked outside our house. She was utterly convinced that somehow, through the blackout, the Germans could see it.

We had ration books but we didn't notice the shortages because locally, everyone knew farmers: in the country you could always get eggs. The RAF boys we'd meet and invite round, Mum would make them bacon and eggs for breakfast, something they couldn't always get elsewhere.

I met Tom Wheatley in the summer of 1940, just before I turned nineteen. There was a local swimming pool that was very popular with anyone in uniform and I first met him there. Then he was posted somewhere near Aylesbury, in Buckinghamshire. He was nineteen, an acting pilot officer in the RAF.

Tom was so sophisticated compared to the Cirencester boys we knew. He'd been to Dulwich Prep School. He came from Kent and while it didn't always run properly, he had a car. His stepfather was a Colonel in the Queen's Regiment. He'd travelled, his grandparents were big landowners. Tom came from a very different world.

On one of our early dates, he took me out for dinner to a lovely inn, the Swan at Bibury, one of the nicest places to eat in the area. I was a little bit nervous because I was still in awe of him, so different to the local boys. While we were eating, Tom discovered something crawling on a piece of lettuce. He just flicked it off the leaf with his fork. To a young innocent country girl, it seemed so clever, knowing how to handle something like that. I was impressed with his sophistication. And I was smitten.

I kept on seeing him through that summer of 1940. A couple of times I travelled to his base and stayed in a hotel nearby on the main street. Then we'd go out at night. I didn't ask my mother whether it was ok to go, which was unusual for me. I just wanted to be with Tom. Back in those days, it was tough having young daughters. There were so many of those attractive young men in uniform around the area. I continued to teach and we'd meet up whenever we could manage it. Or we'd write to each other. It was constant movement for Tom, as he was training he was sent somewhere up in Yorkshire at one stage. By then, he was learning to fly heavy bombers.

I thought I was in love with Tom. I suppose I was a bit of a camp follower as far as he was concerned. We travelled around together whenever we could manage it that next summer of 1941. But something told me, as young as I was, that I had to spend as much time as possible with him. Deep down, instinct told me we wouldn't have very long together. I did go out with other boys, briefly. But after less than eighteen months of seeing each other, we got married in February 1942.

There was no proposal as such. It was more like 'Why don't you marry me and travel with me?' Something casually slipped into the conversation. There was no going down on one knee, that sort of stuff. Life was going too fast.

We all knew that we didn't have time to obey the rules. The war itself made you hurry. Better to make a decision and do something because tomorrow it might be gone. It was a strange time for decision making. In a way, you didn't really think you'd be spending your life with someone. Not when all around you, people you knew were being killed. At one point, I'd gone to see a boy I knew at his base, only to be told he'd had an accident and been killed. The whole thing made you feel as if the ground was constantly shifting under your feet.

We got married in the lovely big St John Baptist Church in Cirencester's market square. Tom's mother and aunt came up from Kent. Tom's stepfather was away fighting in the Middle East. Tom's mother had divorced Tom's real father when Tom was two and remarried. Tom had been born in America, then brought back to Kent.

My parents were a bit nervous about meeting Tom's mother, Nan. It was a very small wedding, I wore a pale green suit with a spray of green and brown orchids. There was no time for a proper honeymoon, we just stayed at a local inn. We only had a few days together. Then he had to go back to his base and I had to go back home because I was still teaching.

There were no married quarters for us on his base as newlyweds. During the war, you couldn't have wives on the base, some of the bases were very dangerous places to be. So when he was moved around, from base to base, we'd have to find different 'homes' for ourselves. I'd left my teaching job soon after we married. I don't think I slept away from Tom the entire time we were married.

What we'd do when he had a new posting was drive to the new area in Tom's 1930s car, a yellow Renault. We'd put my bike on the jump seat at the back and then we'd find a suitable village and split up. He'd go off to the base and I'd get on the bike, go round the village and knock on doors, to see if someone would take us in, rent a room to us in their house.

We'd usually pay about £2 a week for the room. By the time Tom and I met up that evening I'd have usually found someone willing to take us in. There were lots of opportunities to do that during the war because mostly you'd only be staying in the house for a couple of months. And, of course, the money was always welcome.

It was always ordinary, working-class people who took us in. One woman hated us taking a bath. She didn't like her bathroom being messed up. But all the places we stayed in, the people were kind. At one stage, Tom was posted up to Scotland. We found a room in a house where a brother and sister lived, they ran a grocery store together. I was a bit scared of the sister. I always thought she disapproved of me because it was obvious I didn't know much about cooking or housekeeping. But as it turned out, I was wrong.

When Tom was posted to a base in Leaming, just south of York, early in 1943 you could hear the planes because we were so close to the base. In March, he was sent off on his first big bombing raid in a Halifax bomber. On that trip, he was second pilot, the trip was for practice, his first ever trip over Berlin. He'd done some small trips with his own crew but this was a big one. And he went with another crew that night.

After Tom had gone off on the flight, the people we were staying with were so kind to me. They suggested we play cards. Anything to distract me from the sound of all the planes going over until I went to bed that night. And in the morning, their son arrived home from the Army, a young lad with red hair just back from the Middle East.

That morning, there was an unexpected knock at the door. Two people, a minister and a woman volunteer, both from Tom's base. As soon as I saw them, I knew it was my turn. Tom hadn't come back. They were there to tell me, but also to say 'Don't give up hope.' He might have been taken prisoner. They did their best to give me all sorts of hopeful scenarios. 'It's quite possible he wound up landing at another base.' I did my best to hang onto that. But in my heart, I knew that wasn't what had happened. Too many others had been in the same situation.

The first thing I did was call Tom's mother, Nan. She'd just lost her son. But she'd also lost her husband six months before. He was killed at Alamein and they never did find his body. Nan said she'd come to meet me at the station at York and we could then go back to her home in Kent together. The couple I stayed with enlisted their young son with the red hair to accompany me to York on the bus. How he must have hated it, sitting on that bus with a young woman who had just lost her husband. But his parents insisted: they wouldn't let me go alone.

People were so kind to each other then. Some months later, I received a letter from the Scottish woman I thought disapproved of me. It was such a sweet letter, telling me how sorry she was about Tom.

'I always noticed how much you did for him, lighting the fire in the morning and lots of little things like that,' she wrote.

That day in York, Nan and I met up. Her first words to me were: 'I can be brave if you can.' We went back to the house where I'd been staying. That first night, she slept in the bed with me, the same bed her son had slept in the night before he was killed. Later that day, we drove back to her house in Chislehurst, Kent, and I stayed there. Mum and Dad didn't mind, they had Joy around, working at the bank. And they knew Nan had been widowed too.

About three months later, a telegram arrived for me. It was from the King. It said Tom's body had been buried in Antwerp, Belgium. We'd assumed that Tom had been hit by fire over Berlin and come down over the English coast.

It was only in 1970 – when not knowing got the better of me and Joy's husband managed to get some information from the RAF – that we found out the truth. Tom's plane had been brought down by a German fighter plane over Holland on the border with Belgium. Tom, the pilot and one other fellow went down with the plane. When the Germans picked up their bodies, they took them across to Belgium.

I didn't know the men Tom went down with because they weren't his regular crew. But I did then discover that one of the crew was still alive. He sent me a detailed sheet, telling the whole story of Tom's crash. Somehow, this man had managed to bale out, buried his parachute, and spent 24 hours in the countryside. Some people in a farmhouse helped him at first. But their son insisted it was too dangerous to have a British airman in their home. So they gave him up to the Germans. Unfortunately, I never got to meet the man. He died before I could get over to England to meet him.

Staying with Nan helped comfort both of us. But it was the saddest time. I can still remember us going for walks on Chislehurst common with Buffy, Tom's dog. If Buffy saw anyone in uniform he'd gallop up to them eagerly. Then, as soon as he saw it wasn't Tom, he'd trot back to us.

Once we'd found out what had happened to Tom, I started to seriously think about finding some sort of fulltime work. I had found work in a little factory on the outskirts of town, we were freezing batteries and then testing them. I did that for a short time. Then, once we'd got the message about where he was buried, of course we couldn't go to visit his grave until after the war. But it was obvious I had to find some kind of permanent wartime work.

It was around June 1943 that I spotted the advertisement in *Aeroplane* magazine, the same ad that Joy saw. The ATA wanted more pilots, they were willing to train people without any flying experience. In the end, I believe 2000 people wrote off to apply. They took just seventeen. We did have an educational qualification, a Cambridge School Certificate, you took it before age eighteen. Not everyone took it, but that helped our application.

Why did I apply? There were so many reasons. One, I wanted to do something for the war effort. Two, I had become quite fascinated by planes. I knew a lot of flying people. And I would often go for walks in the country and just lie down, looking up at the sky, watching the planes. After Tom died I was always thinking about what had happened to him, in the last few minutes, when he knew the plane was going down.

Again and again, I'd think: 'Did he know it was hopeless?' that sort of thing. You can't help asking yourself those questions.

Nan often said I joined up to fly because I thought I'd be killed too. But this wasn't about a death wish. I saw it as one of the most worthwhile jobs I could possibly have. It seemed natural to me to do my part for the war by flying, once I knew they would accept women without experience. I wasn't reckless about it, not at all.

Nan knew I was applying. We'd all heard about these girls in the ATA who were flying, they'd been in the newspapers. And we'd heard lots about one of these girls who flew through our aunt Nancy, in Hatfield. Nancy's husband was in the Stock Exchange and they had no children. A female pilot called Mary Wilkins had been staying with them, so we all heard about this Mary.

To Joy and I, girls who had already spent a lot of time going out with pilots, dances at the Mess, that sort of thing, it was also a very glamorous life. A case of doing something exciting and interesting. But we knew too there was little chance of getting in.

In those days, Joy thought her older sister was the cat's whiskers. I'm pretty sure she applied because she wanted to do everything I was doing. We didn't look alike and I applied under my married name anyway. But once we'd got in, word soon got around that we were sisters.

My application went in a few weeks before Joy's. And we didn't, for some reason, always know exactly what the other one was doing because Joy had remained at home while I'd gone up to Kent. So there I was, coming out of the station at the White Waltham HQ one day, in the middle of my training and there was my sister Joy, coming in for her initial interview. In the end, she was a couple of classes behind me as we trained.

Most of our training for flying was at Thame, in Oxfordshire. They'd take us by bus every day to a little airfield in Barton-in-the-Clay for flying instruction. It was like a private flying club, all grass fields. We were given twelve hours to solo while we trained. After Barton, we returned to Thame to do cross-country trips, sometimes with an instructor, as we still had a lot to learn. I flew my first Tiger Moth and also the Magister, it had a fixed undercarriage. I joined the ATA in September 1943 and after twelve hours of training I did my first solo flight that November.

Some people, both sexes, didn't make it. They dropped out. There's a lot to flying. You need 'the touch'. I think women were much better when it came to flying the Spitfires. Women have a lighter touch. They're not as ham-fisted.

We had a very thorough training. To take kids like us, starting from scratch, was incredible. When they first showed us a plane and lifted up the cowling covering a Mustang P51, one of the planes which came in towards the end of the war, it was a huge moment. Joy and I had never even been up in the air before.

We were told by the instructor: 'Ask me if there's something you don't understand.' For all I knew that day they showed us the Mustang, they could have uncovered an ice cream truck. Safety, of course, was drilled into all our thinking. And later, when we were actually delivering fighter aircraft to squadrons, the training we received made us very conscious that any accident or incident that could be related to our lack of judgement or care would not be tolerated.

The people training with me were a mixed bunch, a couple of girls from the WAAF, an American woman who had some flying experience but still had to learn our way. Some of the training was at White Waltham, I went there for a conversion course, when we were learning to fly the twin-engine planes like the Anson or Oxford. When it was obvious the weather would not clear and it was impossible to fly, you'd be told, 'It's scrub for the day.' That meant everything was washed out, the weather was too bad to fly.

I earned my wings on 1 March 1944, exactly a year since Tom had been killed. It was satisfying to think that I'd done it, learned to fly, within a year.

Being measured up in London for the navy uniform with gold shoulder strips was another milestone. Now it really was happening. And, of course, once you were out wearing it, you got all sorts of attention. I can still remember walking down Regent Street to find uniformed guys on either side, eager to chat me up.

'Hey, are you Free French?' said one wisescracker.

'No, I'm neither free nor French,' I snapped back.

The uniform opened all kinds of doors socially. After all, there were so few of us female ferry pilots. You'd have thirteen days ferrying and two days off usually, so you wouldn't have much time if you wanted to go to London. Joy and I did very little together during the war, we had separate friends and because we wound up at separate ferry pools, we were either busy flying or making the most of our time off.

I was very conscious of the fact that I was a widow at 22. Although I was far from being the only young woman in that situation. The thing was, I was still quite innocent about the world and its ways. One day I was complaining to an older girl that men always seemed to be pestering me – what should I do about it?

'Oh Yvonne, don't you know? They follow you around because you've been married. And they figure you're up for anything. There's a saying: "You never miss a slice off a cut loaf." That's what it's all about.'

From that point on, until I met my late husband Neil, if a man so much as looked at me I'd think: 'Oh he's got one thing on his mind because he knows I'm a widow.'

Once I'd been told I'd be working from the all-women pool at Cosford, I didn't try to find a billet. I found myself a little apartment on the outskirts of Wolverhampton. What with all the mills up there and all the smoke, it was a lousy place to be. Everyone really wanted to be at Hamble, all the glamorous women were there.

A few were in magazines like *Tatler*, some were socialites. At one stage, I was seconded there for a couple of weeks and I was so impressed with these girls. As an ordinary girl, you couldn't compete with them. They all seemed to have their own car and lovely clothes. I do remember briefly bumming a ride from Diana Barnato Walker from Southampton. I'd been staying in a hotel there and she drove me back to Hamble. I couldn't have been too shy to ask her for a lift!

But I don't think the general atmosphere at the Cosford pool was that different when you were actually waiting to fly. We'd play a lot of bridge while we were waiting. Someone was always sewing something. And you meshed with your own little group, the girls who had trained with you, you'd socialise with them in your time off. I loved meeting new people. As for discrimination because we were female, I didn't encounter it from our men in the ATA. Mostly, they were a bit older, too old for the RAF. But there was no resentment from them.

There were ATA girls who were killed. One of them was a flight engineer. I didn't know any of them well enough to feel I'd lost a friend, you didn't get to meet everyone who flew for ATA, naturally.

I did become very friendly with a girl who joined at the same time as me, Audrey Morgan. Her father had a flat in London and sometimes he'd organise small groups of American servicemen to escort us whenever we had a couple of nights off and could take the train there. We'd be in small groups of eight or ten, dinner dancing in the West End to Edmundo Ross at places like the Dorchester, the Brevet Club. Joy and I never really got the smoking habit. But I'd buy Black Balkan Sobranies with a gold tip, just to hold with a drink, in an attempt to look more sophisticated.

The whole time I was flying, I did everything the way I had been taught. I was never going to take any chances. We were not there to break or wreck aircraft. But I did have one accident with a Spitfire. It was an error of judgement. I held off a little bit too high on landing it. I was 8ft above the runway, instead of 3ft. Coming in, it dropped a little too heavily and I burst the right tyre as it slewed around when it touched the runway.

Technically, it wasn't a crash; I'd landed on both wheels. I'd damaged a tip of the wing and they fixed it. But I was extra cautious after that. We were there to get the plane from A to B and that was it. Perhaps I'd have been allowed one more mistake after my tyre incident but the report came back: pilot error. If I'd had two or more of those they'd have started looking at me very seriously. The planes cost thousands, even in those days, and a lot of the time we were bringing in new planes from the factories. At one point, we were taking Seafires into a naval base just off the south coast. Whenever I took a plane at this base, I always ran out of runway.

I just couldn't figure it out. I had so much trouble with that runway, it was narrow and short. But of course, it was used by the pilots to practise landing on a ship. They knew it was a shortened runway and got used to that. But little old me, I just didn't know.

If it hadn't been for the heavy parachute we had to take with us if we were ferrying a fighter plane like the Spit, fate might have taken a different turn for me. These parachutes weighed about 10 or 12lb and I'd always just sling it over my shoulder. No one ever offered to carry it for me. Why should they? We were healthy girls and we were capable of doing the job.

But one day, I had an accident on the ground. I jumped out of a field car that was taking us around the airfield to the planes and stupidly, with the parachute on my shoulder, the heavy weight on my shoulder twisted my ankle as I jumped. I couldn't work, so I was sent off on leave to stay with my parents in Cirencester.

My father loved horses, so one day he took me with him to the race track at Cheltenham. There we were, sitting with a group of my father's friends, when I got up to place a bet. Standing right behind me was a tall, handsome man in uniform. He was with a group of other flyers from the Royal Canadian Air Force. We started talking. Then he handed me a piece of paper. He'd written: 'Hot Tip', followed by his name and address. He was stationed nearby at Cheltenham.

Neil MacDonald had been born in Scotland, taken over to America at the age of three and settled in New York State. Yet he still retained a Scottish accent. And he'd joined the Canadian Air Force because the Americans wouldn't take him: technically he was still British.

I tucked the little slip of paper into my bag. Then I went back to my father and his friends. My father, for some reason, didn't like Americans. Or Canadians come to that. And he'd spotted me chatting to Neil. To him, these were people from another planet. A lot of people thought like that. 'What on earth are you doing, talking to that Canadian?' he growled.

'Oh, we were just talking about the horses, Dad,' I told him airily.

Back at work at Cosford, the next time I had a plane to deliver in Neil's area, I managed to stop off at the airfield he'd written down on the piece of paper. He wasn't at his base, so I left him a message.

Later, Neil told me that when he came back he was handed my message with the comment 'Hey Neil, there was an ATA Tomato looking for you today.' Then Neil phoned me. And we started from there.

Neil was handsome, quiet and quite shy. I think he was a bit in awe of me at first, a female pilot who'd already been widowed. And, to be honest, I was still thinking about Tom. A lot. Yet by now it was obvious that the tide had turned in the war, that soon it would be all over. Neil would come to visit us when I was on leave at Cirencester. At first, my father didn't approve. 'Foreigners again,' he'd say, because Joy, of course, was engaged to George, who was from Czechoslovakia. But once he got to know Neil, he loved him. Neil was that sort of person.

We didn't actually talk about marriage until we'd decided to do it. By now, I was starting to think it might be good to leave England after the war was over and Neil was obviously heading back home across the Atlantic. And so we were married in Darlington in Yorkshire in May 1945. We just went and did it. I admit, I wept a few tears beforehand. I wasn't really sure I was doing it for the best. I wanted to marry Neil. But I was also looking for change after all that had happened.

I got out of ATA in June, I was sad that it was all over. The last plane that I ever flew was a Spitfire, from Scotland down to Yorkshire, though I didn't know at the time it was my last flight. Everything was closing down by then. It really was like resigning from a job you loved, a place where there was a lot of camaraderie.

Some of the airfields held little parties. After Cosford had closed, I ended up working briefly at Sherborn in Elmet in the West Midlands. Our HQ was a sort of farmhouse.

We didn't all leave on the same day, it just petered out, a little party at each base, nothing organised. People just drifted off. When you came in one morning and found that someone else had left, all you could think of was the future. I had known the flying wouldn't lead to anything, though I would have liked to continue flying. But we all knew there were so many wanting to do just that, too many people looking for too few jobs. There were just too many trained service pilots out there.

When Japan surrendered in August, Neil and I went up to London by train and had a few days there. We were outside the Palace, waving and shouting with everyone else going crazy in the streets.

By now, I knew I'd probably be leaving England. I travelled around a little bit with Neil to a few bases. He'd wanted to stay in the service, keep flying, make it a career, but again, too many people had the same idea. So he'd decided to go back to America, get a job as soon as possible, then I could join him. Already pregnant with our first child, Wendy, I went back to my parents' home in Cirencester and Wendy was born there in April 1946. We finally flew off to join Neil in September that year.

Once we'd arrived, Neil took us to meet his family in New York State. It wasn't a great situation. His mother was unwell. We weren't sure what to do. But after a few months we realised we'd probably be better off to strike out, not to remain in New York State.

By this time, Neil decided he'd go back to school to do business studies. So he'd applied to study at McGill University in Montreal. And so we found ourselves living there, all married students, housed together in Nissen type hut buildings, many of us with children. We had two rooms in this big building with its central dining hall. We had $128 a month from the Canadian Government. There were hundreds of couples like us, all living together, eating communally.

At one point, Tom's mother Nan came over to visit and stopped with us for a couple of nights. She always kept an eye on me. And we had a very nice relationship which lasted until she died aged 90.

Our first son, Peter, was born in Montreal in 1950, right in the middle of Neil's business degree. By then we'd moved out of the big building into an apartment and I got a job, a little bit of waitressing at night. All the men studied at night while the children were in bed, so me and two other women (their husbands were studying medicine) were able to do some part-time evening waitressing. We'd all catch the bus together to take us to the restaurant in a big hotel.

Before Peter arrived, I'd managed to get a holiday in England in 1948. I took Wendy with me and Joy had just come back from Czechoslovakia with her baby son so there we were with our parents and our babies.

By 1952, Neil's studies had finished and we went to live in Connecticut. Neil had been offered a very good job as an executive with a large insurance company. So we started out again, with our two children, renting a place in West Hertford. I can still remember Neil saying: 'If I stay with this company I might make $10,000 a year one day.' He was so thrilled to get that job after the years of studying.

Neil and I went on to have five children, four boys, one girl. Five is a lot. But I always wanted five kids though I didn't know what it would be like to bring up that many children.

We moved a few times as Neil's career progressed and eventually built a lovely big house near a country club with tennis, swimming, golf on hand. It was a good life. I played tennis every day, I've only recently stopped. And I did a lot of volunteer work for children's services. At one point I drove an ambulance and when the children were older I belonged to the Connecticut Prison Association. We'd take youngsters who were in reform school out for the day.

I had a wonderful husband who spoiled me, really. I'd go to England every September for a big ATA reunion, people were always surprised to see me and Neil came with me a couple of times. But he didn't object when I started going alone, he didn't keep up with his own wartime reunions. Once the war was over, that was it for him.

I didn't have any au pairs or anyone to help me with the children: America runs for children but I tried to keep things a little bit English and a little bit more disciplined. I didn't always agree with the way people in America brought up their kids. It was all quite different from the way Joy and I had been brought up.

Yet I was very satisfied with my life. I was never homesick in the early years because there were a lot of Scottish couples in the town we lived in. And anyway, if I wanted home, I could pop over any time. And the children came with me. Neil was a bit of a homebody. He spent a lot of time travelling for his job. Sometimes I'd be alone for four or five weeks at a time. And nine times out of ten we'd have a heavy winter in Connecticut and I'd be out there, shovelling snow while he'd be flying off to California. Though there were times when the wives would accompany their husbands, so I saw plenty of other places: California, Bermuda, Puerto Rico, Hawaii.

We were never short of money. We weren't rolling in it. But it was a very comfortable life. At one stage, I sold real estate in Connecticut for some years.

I didn't ever fly again. I plunged right into another life. In the 1950s, when I was in England visiting some ATA friends, I looked up Monique Agazarian, who set up Island Air Services at Heathrow Airport, running pleasure flights over London until the end of the decade. I went up with Monique one day. I couldn't have flown solo because I didn't have a pilot's licence but it was wonderful to fly with her. And I always kept in touch with Audrey Morgan, she also continued to fly on the south coast.

My navigation skills came in useful later when we'd go sailing sometimes on the East Coast of Massachusetts. I did a lot of sailing on a 65ft ketch and I'd steer this: I found I could still hold a course.

Neil decided to retire at 60 and we moved to Cape Cod, a town called Osterville, full of tennis players and young people. Perhaps he should have stayed working a bit longer, he loved his job and missed it but we bought a place in Florida too, a second home in the sunshine. Though I wasn't over-fond of Florida, terrible drivers, mostly old ladies who can't see over the wheel.

Neil died in 2001 and, sadly, two of our boys died from cancer after that. Robert died in 2010 aged 53 and David died at 46 in 2006. Today, my sons Peter and John live close by on the Cape and my daughter Wendy is in Connecticut. I have seven grandchildren and two great-grandchildren.

I'm sure the whole experience I had during the war made a lot of difference to the way I eventually turned out. It toughened us a little bit, put steel in the backbone.

I'm not a spiritual person. But once you've come through something like flying in wartime – and losing a husband at such a young age – nothing can get you down very much. A lot of people here in Cape Cod don't even know I was in the Second World War. Or what I did.

Flying the Spitfire was a kind of freedom you never get any other way.

More than anything, with the Spit, it was always as if you had wings sewn on your back. That was exactly how it felt. It was so manoeuvrable. Once, on a cloudy, rainy day, I ran my right wing through a rain cloud: rain on the right wing, on the left there was sunshine. You could do almost anything with those planes. I'm so lucky to have had that experience.

Sometimes, when you were landing the Spitfire at dusk – we were supposed to land 20 minutes before dusk – when it would just be starting to get dark, you felt it was almost as if you could play with the whole world. I can only describe it as an otherworldly feeling.

When I think about that feeling, I remember that very famous poem, 'High Flight', written by John Gillespie Magee. He was nineteen when he was killed in Lincolnshire in 1941, flying a Spitfire for the Royal Canadian Air Force. The words of the poem are inscribed on his tombstone: 'Oh! I have slipped the surly bonds of earth – put out my hand and touched the face of God.'

Time has given it all such a patina, time has glorified everything, of course. I was always amazed to be up there to start with. But I really do think it was a wonderful job that we did.

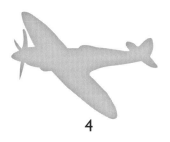

4

MOLLY ROSE

Molly was born in Cambridge in November 1920. She joined the ATA on 16 September 1942, leaving on 25 May 1945 as a 1st Officer. She delivered 486 planes and flew 36 different types of aircraft.

The word 'remarkable' immediately springs to mind when meeting Molly Rose in her comfortable early eighteenth-century Georgian home in a pretty Cotswolds village.

The seventh child of a family of eight children, she grew up in a well heeled environment where flying was part of the family business. Yet hers was no aristocratic background. Her father, David Gregory Marshall, was very much a self made individual. And a man of vision. Molly's father started his working life at fourteen as a kitchen hand. But with amazing perspicacity, he spotted the potential of the internal combustion engine at the dawn of the twentieth century. What started out as a tiny garage and car sales centre run by Molly's father and her brother Arthur went on, over time, to become Marshalls of Cambridge, an internationally renowned aerospace engineering company.

Today, the Marshall Group of Companies has five divisions: Marshall Aerospace, Marshall Land Systems, Marshall Motor Holdings, Marshall Airport Properties and Cambridge Airport,

3 miles outside the city of Cambridge. The Group has an annual turnover of £985 million and 4200 employees.

Modest to a fault, continuously hard working into her nineties, and definitely not prone to self aggrandisement – 'for 70 years no one asked about it and you didn't even think of talking about it' – was her comment on the renewed interest in the ATA women pilots, Molly's wartime ATA memories and those of her late husband Bernard (as a prisoner of war in Germany) are very much part of British history. They can be found in recordings at London's Imperial War Museum, with other recordings of ATA pilots.

After the war, her flying years were over; Molly concentrated on raising her family of three sons and working tirelessly in the community as a JP and magistrate. She was awarded an OBE in 1989 for services to Oxford and she has continued to remain active within the community.

'The Spitfire was a Woman's Plane'

I was the seventh child of a family of eight. The eldest, my brother Arthur, was born in 1903. The youngest, my sister Brenda, was born in 1927. My father had worked his way up from working in the kitchens of Trinity College, Cambridge to be Manager of the exclusive Pitt Club, the Cambridge undergraduate social club, by the time he reached his twenties.

In 1906 he took my mother Maud on a trip to Paris, where he realised that the French were very much ahead of us in the development of the internal combustion engine. There were very few cars on the road in Britain at that time. But Paris already had motor buses. So he promptly decided that was the future.

When he got back to Cambridge he bought two cars which could be hired out, chauffeur driven, for the undergraduate members of the Pitt Club – or anyone else willing to pay to hire them. The cars were a Belgian-made Metallurgique and a French Cottin Desgouttes.

Then he started a garage offering sales and service, selling Rolls-Royce, Daimler and Bugatti. It was called the Brunswick Motor Car Company. And by the time I arrived in 1920, my brother Arthur was already starting to be interested in the possibilities of aviation and developing the car business around it.

I must have been about six years old when Arthur learned to fly in Norwich after finishing his engineering studies at Jesus College, Cambridge. I don't think my mother knew he was going to learn – it was very unusual – but my father, of course, encouraged this. Arthur learned to fly on a Gypsy Moth (the same plane I eventually learned to fly on) and he got his 'B' licence very quickly. Very soon he'd bought his own Gypsy Moth. It was tethered behind our home on the edge of Cambridge, on the Newmarket Road. A few years later, my father and brother established the Marshall Flying School there – and gradually the aviation business expanded.

Our family house was called White Hill. It had big tennis courts and orchards. It was vast, you ran round from one point of warmth to another. We had two maids, a cook and a housemaid. And we all got on incredibly well. I realise now how fortunate I was in my childhood: you do run across families who don't have happy home lives.

My eldest sister, Margery, twelve years older than me, flew in the King's Cup Air Race with my brother at one stage. She learned to fly but she never had a licence. So you see, as far as I was concerned, flying was part of our life. As a little girl, if Arthur was going somewhere in the plane, he wouldn't mind taking me.

'Come on,' he'd say, 'Jump in!' He was the only brother in a house of six sisters – our other brother Ronald had died at fifteen months from meningitis – so he was always looked up to by the girls.

I'd jump in with glee, often in a thin summer frock, so I'd wind up getting very cold – the cockpit was open, there was no cover whatsoever – when we'd fly off somewhere close like Newmarket. Aviation then was new. You could land anywhere.

In the summer the family would go to Heacham, on the Norfolk Coast for a month and he'd fly down to join us. Flying was part of the family business so it sort of fitted into our life. As was having a car – the car and the plane were always available to us.

One of my most vivid memories of childhood is when I was about eight or nine, sitting in the front cockpit of my brother's plane. You talked through a tube, wearing a helmet with earphones which was plugged into the speaking tube coming from the other cockpit, so you could communicate. It was so exciting, the newest thing, being able to get places so quickly. It was seen as fun. But not dangerous. At that young age – and indeed later on, when I was in the ATA – I wasn't frightened of anything.

The sad thing was my mother Maud died when I was ten. She had a stroke. She was just 52 and my youngest sister, Brenda was three. It was a tremendous sadness for everyone. But equally, in those days, people were very brave about things. They didn't collapse in a heap. I can still remember crying about it all one morning to be told by an older sister: 'Molly, we don't *do* that, it'll upset Daddy.' So you didn't do it.

It was a tremendous responsibility for my father. By then, my brother Arthur had married, so there were six girls living at home, though Margery, the eldest, was engaged and got married soon afterwards. She became a secretary for the family business.

My other sister Violet also trained in secretarial work. She wound up finishing her schooling in Switzerland so she housekept for us all after that. My sister Dorothy went off to University at Liverpool and trained to be a games and gym mistress. And my sister Mary was educated at St Mary's Convent, Paston House, in Cambridge and the Convent of the Sacred Heart in Brighton, followed by a secretarial course.

As for me, I too went to Paston House as a day girl until I was twelve, then I went to boarding school, Slepe Hall in St Ives, Huntingdonshire, until I was sixteen. To this day, I have no idea how my father managed to finance it all. But he did. And he was very keen for us as women to be independent, he reckoned his daughters should be trained for something. The thinking was: 'You may marry but people die – and you could get into a situation where you need to earn.' And he was also very serious about education: 'The one thing in life you can never take away from someone is their education.'

By sixteen, I'd already had flying lessons. I was home one term from boarding school and my father gave me lessons: I didn't have to nag him to let me fly. Not that I'd have got anywhere if I had. You didn't question anyone's authority then.

Around that time my father took me to Paris by boat train to see the finishing school he'd chosen for me. I spent January to July 1937 there. We were meant to speak French all the time. But of course, we didn't. If a chaperone was around, you spoke French and you had classes in French literature, culture, trips to the opera, riding in the Bois du Boulogne.

There were about 20 girls, all English. Paris was very exciting for us though we didn't know about all the naughty places. We were incredibly innocent then. For instance, I'd never run across women who preferred other women at that stage. But I can remember one of the chaperones, none of us wanted to sit next to her in a taxi. The word went round the group not to sit with her – yet I had no idea of the real reason why.

The idea was for us to be fluent in French. I'd still have piano lessons and fortunately, I am fairly musical. What I didn't know then, of course, was that music was eventually to play a big part in my life, even though we were not a particularly musical family.

But at that stage of life, as young girls you thought of marriage, you wanted to be married. We saw life as something where everything fitted in very neatly. Of course, by then there were very loud rumblings of what was to come in Europe, though we didn't really notice it. You didn't get information then in the way you do now. Unless you made a point of following the news in the papers and the radio, you were not aware. My father didn't talk to us about international politics either.

By the time I got back from Paris, two of my sisters, Violet and Mary, were married. The general idea was that I'd take over and run the household for my father. But in fact, he'd found a very capable housekeeper. Very wisely he saw I wouldn't be very good at it.

One day, my father asked me if I wanted to go flying. Of course, I was all for this idea. But he wondered if it might not be a good idea for me to actually learn how planes worked.

'Hmm, that's a novel idea. Can I think about it?' was my response. I wasn't sure what this meant. But by the next morning, I told him yes. I realised it was a brilliant idea.

'OK, start Monday. I've already got your overalls,' was his response.

By now, the aerodrome hangar had moved from behind our home and became – and still is – the Cambridge aerodrome. It was owned by my father and brother, but my brother ran it. So I started cycling up the road every day to learn more about the planes. They were teaching people to fly there – in single-engine, open cockpit Tiger Moths.

And that was how, in 1938, I learned how to be a ground engineer, working on the aircraft, the first female engineering trainee. If you work for the family firm, you have to work twice as hard to prove you're not getting any privileges. I reported for work right on the dot. And I didn't take days off. Yet I was very lucky. I found it all fascinating. I had caught my father's fascination with the internal combustion engine.

I'd strip engines down, do all sorts of maintenance on them. Sometimes you'd strip them down and replace component parts. I'd also have to be on duty with night flying, just in case there was a heavy landing. If this happened, you had to inspect the airframe to make sure it was safe enough to continue flying.

Of course, I was the only woman working on the hangar floor. Yet the men there were good to me and I've got a fairly good sense of humour. If I got stuck with a bolt or a screw that wouldn't budge, they'd always help me.

On one occasion I was rewiring a Gypsy Moth, bent double with my head in the cockpit and I felt a playful flick on the behind. I roared with laughter. If I'd been prim or pulled rank, it wouldn't have gone down well. And I was enjoying the work, taking engines to piece and completely de-coking them. Though it ruined my hands for life.

At the time, I had a good social life too. Soon after I came back from Paris, the wife of the Master of St Catherine's College, Oxford rang my father and asked if I'd like to go to supper there one Sunday. I had a friend staying that weekend who'd been at the school in Paris with me. My father explained all this to her. 'All the better, tell her to bring her friend.'

By then, I'd been given a little Austin 7 to run around. I'd passed my driving test at seventeen. So we drove to the Masters' Lodge. The guests were two other girls and 23 young men, all undergraduates at St Catherine's.

It was an eventful supper. For that evening, I met Bernard Rose, a musician, playing keyboard and French horn, up for his fourth year. He'd already taken two degrees in music there and was staying up to take another one. I was nearly 18. He was 22.

Towards the end of the evening, a list was passed to Bernard asking if he was going to a dance later that year. Would he be bringing a partner?

'Oh Molly, you will come, won't you?' our hostess said. So several weeks later in November, I turned up again at the Masters' Lodge, in full evening dress, leaving my little car in the garage a quarter of a mile away.

At that point, I wasn't particularly interested in Bernard Rose. The minute I arrived, a very good looking chap called Harry McQuaid took me over and we danced, dance after dance, laughing and talking. At around 9.30pm Bernard appeared, tapped Harry on the shoulder saying 'Thanks, old boy,' and took over. Bernard, complete with smart dinner jacket, was late because he'd been conducting the University orchestra.

'Harry's looked after you,' he told me. 'And he's done a good job.' He'd actually planned the whole thing!

In my memory, that night in November 1938 was a lovely evening, dancing to a three-piece orchestra, chatting, dance after dance. And as I got my coat to leave, Bernard wanted to escort me to my car. But by the time we'd walked to the car, he realised something: he was locked out of St Catherine's and he didn't have a key. And so our first date ended with him climbing up a lamppost to get back in.

Driving home that night, I felt so good. He'd made me feel special somehow. He was good looking, he danced well and he was great fun to be with: what more did I want? And so we started seeing each other regularly through the following year. In July 1939, he got a job at Queen's College, Oxford as Organist and Fellow in Music. By September 1939, he was tutoring in music. This meant he had a phone in his room. So if he happened to hear I'd gone out with someone else, he'd ring me, wanting to know if I'd had a good evening.

Of course, the war was overshadowing everything. By this time my father was spending a lot of time down at our house in Hove, Sussex. He owned a small string of horses there and that September weekend when war broke out, I'd driven my father and youngest sister down to Sussex in a Buick; we were planning to ride on the Sussex Downs on the Sunday morning. We took a radio with us as we rode up to the Downs, so we could listen to the Prime Minister's announcement. We knew bad news was coming. When, at 11.00am, Neville Chamberlain said: 'We are at war with Germany,' there we all were, on horseback, trying to take it all in.

When the speech finished my father said we should all ride off in different directions. He wanted to be on his own. He'd known war (he'd won an MBE in 1918 for his war work with the Ministry of Munitions at Woolwich Arsenal). He believed this news was something we ought to take in very seriously. He told us: 'In a family as large as ours, we shan't all come through this.' So we all rode off alone for an hour.

I knew he was probably right. You weren't tearful, you didn't panic. Displaying emotion simply wasn't done, though I think now that was how people got through it all. But of course, you had no idea what was going to happen.

That night, we went back to Cambridge and the same night, the sirens went off. We had already been equipped with gas masks. And we didn't go down to our cellar. But thankfully the gas masks were never used.

As for me and Bernard, I was still working at the aerodrome. I wasn't being paid because I already had an allowance of £250 a year from my father. And my father liked Bernard very much. Just like my father, Bernard was an extremely slow eater, a quick way to my father's heart!

By then, Bernard had already been to our home a great deal. He came from a farming family in Hertfordshire but his father had died young from peritonitis at the age of 33. It was tragic: he'd been too busy working and wouldn't see a doctor until it was too late. So my mother-in-law to be had been left with three children to raise. They then went to live in Salisbury. His mother was very musical and would sing in choirs, so Bernard became a chorister at Salisbury and that started his musical career.

Bernard's marriage proposal came by phone. He was staying with some friends and he'd kept talking to them about me and they'd said: 'Bernard, you'd better get on with it then'. There and then, he'd rung me at White Hill from their house.

'Molly, they say I'm being ridiculous. I'd better get on and marry you.' I think he thought that if he went to my father first, he'd be expected to talk about how he was going to support me – and at the time, academics were not paid very much. In the end, we both went to see my father in Hove and he was fine. As for me, I was delighted. The proposal didn't come as a real surprise.

We were married at Hove Parish Church on 23 December 1939 with a reception at the Royal Pavilion in Brighton. I was just 19, Bernard was 23.

There was no question of getting married in white in wartime, it wouldn't have been right. I had a beautiful dress and jacket made for me by couture designer Digby Morton. It was a lovely dark blue light wool with velvet appliqué on the hips and a short jacket with velvet trim, accompanied by a hat made by John Boyd. Over my shoulders I wore a pair of blue fox furs. This became my best outfit for years. [Morton also designed the Women's Voluntary Service uniform that same year.] It was Advent and churches don't have flowers at Advent, so I carried a small bouquet of freesias and carnations.

We started married life in a small flat in Oxford in Norham Gardens. Bernard volunteered but he wasn't called up until September 1940. He was sent out to Warminster in Wiltshire as a trooper in the Royal Armoured Corps; I'd travel down there on weekends when I could but once he was called up, I went back to the aerodrome and my job as a ground engineer, living in Cambridge with my brother and his wife.

I was working very hard on the Tiger Moths and other aircraft were being brought to the aerodrome to be repaired from crashes. We worked on whatever came in. It was certainly war work. I'd cycle to the aerodrome just before 8.00am and work until evening, cycling home in the blackout.

While Bernard was still in training, I'd manage to drive down to see him about once a month, if I could save up enough petrol. There wasn't any time to sit around worrying what might happen in the future: you were too busy coping with day-to-day life.

Until the early part of 1942, Bernard had been commissioned into the Northamptonshire Yeomanry and the regiment came up to just outside Cambridge, so we could see a lot of each other. But then two dramatic events happened around the same time: my father, out riding an Arab horse brought back from Egypt, had a sudden brain haemorrhage. He slipped from the horse. The horse stayed with him until they found him. He was gone, aged 69.

Just before this, Bernard, now a squadron leader, had been told by a Corporal that he would not, under any circumstances, wash down his tank with diesel oil to make it shine. He told Bernard his brother had been sunk twice in the Atlantic while bringing diesel oil over from the US – he thought it was pointless wasting the oil on the exterior of the tank.

Bernard went to his Colonel. 'I've got mutiny in my troop sir.' And then he told him the story. 'And I totally agree with him, sir.'

'You'd better leave the Regiment,' said the Colonel. In the end, Bernard and two other men left the Regiment and were sent to Catterick, where they needed a pool of officers to send out to the Middle East.

I'd lost my father. And now my husband was being posted overseas. I went up to Catterick by train to wave him off on the boat. Back in Cambridge, there were several letters waiting for me. One was from the Air Transport Auxiliary. I was no. 98 on their list of females with pilots' licences. They wanted to know if I was interested in joining them.

I already knew about ATA and that women were ferrying planes. I also had no idea how long I would be parted from Bernard. A change of career, I reasoned, was a very good idea.

My ATA interview at White Waltham was pretty straightforward. They needed me. But I hadn't said anything to Bernard about hoping to be a ferry pilot. Eventually, I was able to get a cable to him to Cairo, Egypt. My cable was short and to the point.

'I've joined the ATA. Hope you don't mind.' In fact, I had no idea if Bernard would be concerned about me flying in the war because we'd never discussed it.

I also posted a couple of photos of myself to him in Cairo. I thought it might soften the blow, so I'd gone to a well known society photographer of the time in London, Dorothy Wilding. 'Let's make him think it's glamorous,' I said. I think, when he got them, he realised his wife was more attractive than he'd realised.

By then, ATA had a very efficient way of training people who were coming to them. I was asked to report to Luton for my test flight on a Tiger Moth, if people with existing flying experience needed training, it could take place there. Then I was billeted with a very nice woman at Luton. She was a milliner, in those days they used to make a lot of hats in the area.

The day I joined the ATA I met up with a girl who was also joining, Betty McDougall. Betty was a few years older than me. She had been an art teacher in Scotland. She'd won a scholarship to learn to fly at Renfrew. And she'd had a great battle with the local education authority to be released to fly. We became great friends and she'd sometimes come to stay with me and my family in Cambridge. Her billet, as it turned out, was round the corner to mine, so we'd catch the same bus each day to the Luton airfield, just a little grass airfield at the time.

At first, I was flying a Pussmoth, a single-engine light aircraft as a run-in. Then I went onto flying a single-engined Harvard, much faster, much more powerful. These Harvards had twin cockpits so you learned to fly the Harvard with an instructor. After that, you were sent off in a Hurricane – and that *was* exciting. In those days, once you were airborne you could fly higher or lower. At that time, no one minded. And you didn't have to keep on one patch. You could take the plane away a bit and get used to the 'feel' of the aircraft. Flying was freer then. I can't tell you how different it was from flying nowadays.

You'd think: 'this aircraft is terrific because of its power and the wonderful feeling of being in charge of this very powerful machine.' That's great. But then, of course, you've got to land it. So you'd join the circuit around the aerodrome and then go through your cockpit routine, putting the wheels down and lining it up to come in and land. And if all was clear and you could land, you'd get a ground light from the signals officer on the ground.

With the Hurricane, however, you're coming in much faster. And if you hadn't been in one before, you hoped like mad you'd get it right. In landing, you'd have to judge to get it to exactly the right height above the ground, so you can cut the engine and land. Get it wrong and you'd go bouncing along. It's the same process in any aircraft. When you actually land, you've got to cut the engine. That first Hurricane flight, I felt very hopeful. And managed to land it perfectly.

Then I was let loose to start ferrying all the single-seater fighters, the Spitfires, Tempests, Typhoons. The Hurricane was more of a work horse, the Germans were more scared of the Spitfires because they could maneouvre so neatly.

But once you did the ferrying of the single-engine craft you went back into school to learn to fly the light twin-engine aircraft, first the Oxford and then the Ansons, Wellingtons and that category.

Then after you'd done a certain amount of ferrying on those aircraft you had tuition on the Hudson, a heavy twin-engine bomber.

You had to have an engineer with you on that, because you couldn't put the landing gear down from the cockpit. There were female engineers. I always felt a bit sorry for the engineers because they had to go up with pilots who might not have flown that particular type of plane before.

After my training at Luton and White Waltham, I'd been sent to work from the all-women ferry pool at Hamble. I thought it was going to be jolly dull. I was totally wrong. There was a pool of about 30 women pilots literally from all over the world: a real League of Nations. And there was a big age difference in the group. One woman, Lois Butler was already a grandmother.

By this time, there were shortages, of course. Everyone was short of food. You did what you could with what you had. As for clothes, having had a trousseau when we married – at that time you could still get things – I didn't buy any more clothes and then, of course, being in uniform most of the time meant clothes were not a problem. It was such a smart uniform, navy blue jacket, blue shirt, navy tie, specially fitted at Austin Reed in London. The uniforms were really livery, you were meant to hand them in. I was a 3rd Officer, one gold bar on my epaulette. I was so proud of that. [Molly was eventually promoted to 1st Officer.]

The day's routine went like this. You reported at 9.00am to the ops office, got your programme for the day. You'd get a set of chits telling you which aircraft you'd be taking. If it was a plane you hadn't flown before, you'd get handling notes which, if you were lucky, you'd get a chance to look at on the way. You always had a loose leaf book with a printed set of salient features of all the aircraft you'd be flying.

When your job started at an aerodrome, we had taxi aircraft to take us from Hamble to wherever we were taking the first plane from; if three of us were going anywhere in a taxi, it was a

Fairchild single-engine (three passengers and a pilot). If there were more of us, we'd go in a twin-engine Anson (which could take eight passengers). The taxi was usually a 20-minute hop and usually a very relaxed start to the day's work; all the pilots took it in turns to fly the taxi, on occasion I'd do the taxi.

When you ferried, you had a compass on the plane. But you always consulted the Met Office at every aerodrome before take-off. The extraordinary thing was, although they'd only be getting information from around the British Isles, you'd bet your bottom dollar they'd get it right.

On some of the planes you had an altimeter calibrated from the aerodrome you had just left. So if you were flying over mountains, it was really no help. And the Cotswolds area could be hairy to fly over because some of the hills are quite high. It was the same in Yorkshire and Central Scotland – anywhere where there were hills was dodgy.

The only time I had a prang was in a Swordfish, one of the Fleet Air Arm craft. I was flying it north over the Wrekin when the engine cut out completely. I tried changing tanks. I tried pushing and pulling everything in sight but I could not restart the engine.

I was flying between 1000 and 2000ft. So there wasn't much time to make up my mind what to do next. I decided I'd have to make a forced landing and looked around for a suitable field. But everything I saw was the size of a pocket hanky.

Then I spotted one that seemed a bit bigger. But what I didn't know was that it was sloping downhill. And the aircraft had no brakes. So I came down – and went through a hedge and right into a field beyond. There was a boy there, ploughing a field with a couple of horses. I went down hard. I missed him but it turned the plane over and there I was, hanging onto the straps. I don't like to think what my language was at that moment. Yet I managed to release myself gently from the straps and crawled out.

I left him in charge of the plane while I went to the farmhouse to ring base. Once I'd told them what happened, they contacted Cosford (the other all-female pool) and eventually they sent a car to pick me up.

The funny thing was, there was some security equipment on the aircraft. So the Cosford people had to mount guard on it. Back at Cosford, I was checked out. Physically, I was incredibly lucky, a bruise or two here or there. Then I rang my brother-in-law, my sister Margaret's husband, Monty Fry. He was stationed at RAF Cosford. He turned up to collect me with two bikes. So we cycled out to a restaurant and had dinner together. The next day I was back at Hamble. I told Bernard the news in an airmail letter. By this time, he was in North Africa.

I was just 22 when I joined the ATA, at that age you don't doubt your own capabilities. But the one time I probably shocked myself was taking off from the aircraft factory at Eastleigh, near Southampton, in a Spitfire.

I was ferrying it north, the weather was slightly dodgy. It seemed to be the sort of cloud you could get under or over. I was going over the Cotswolds. As I've said, you didn't know what the ground was underneath you. Suddenly I was into bad cloud.

I tried going under it; and came face to face with one of the Cotswold Hills.

Fortunately for me, I had just enough power to pull the nose back and gain height fast. And I just got over the hill. And I mean 'just'. Thank God for power. That incident in the Spitfire made me very respectful of weather. But of all the planes I flew, my favourite had to be the Spitfire, you could dance with them.

Flying the Spitfire was rather like putting on an overcoat: you fitted. It was a woman's plane. And you always had to take a parachute with you, there was nothing else for you to sit on. Not that we had any training in the use of the parachute. You knew that if you had to bale out, the form was count three – and pull the string. You also took a small overnight holdall everywhere you were going, just in case you wound up doing an overnight somewhere.

I spent three years working at the ferry pool and I had a lot of friends there, it was a very easy-going pool. We all got on well. If there were fights or rows between women, I never noticed them. There were bad moments when someone was killed flying. Mostly, you wouldn't know about such things until you reported for work in the morning.

I had a husband I was waiting for, I very much wanted the war to be over, to be reunited with him. But the advent of D-Day in the summer of 1944, for me, brought the kind of news you hope you won't ever receive– Bernard was missing, presumed killed.

As a tank commander with the Royal Armoured Corps 4th County of London Yeomanry, he was in the first wave of tanks advancing on Villers Bocage, France, after the Normandy landings in June.

After D-Day I got a letter from a friend in Bernard's regiment. The letter said he'd seen Bernard's tank burn up and that no one could have got out of it. But what we didn't know at the time was that Bernard was already out of his tank. He was trying to get someone else out of another burning tank. It was an act that saved his life.

I asked my Commanding Officer, Margot Gore, if I could go to London to the Red Cross, in case they had any information. They had no news. Back at Hamble, I rang Margot Gore to tell her the news. But I knew I wanted to get back to work. And she agreed it was the best thing to do. Sitting around, waiting for news, was no tonic for anyone. My sisters were marvellous. They tried to make sure that one of them was around at all times when I wasn't working. That helped a lot.

I received a formal letter from the War Office saying my husband was missing. A fortnight later came another letter. It said he was missing, believed killed on 13 June. It was the worst possible news anyone could hear. But I felt very strongly that I would know if anything had happened to Bernard. And that belief, I think, saved me. I didn't despair. I felt more sorry for his mother, helping out in a canteen near where she lived. She had all day to worry about her son. But when you're flying, you're so occupied with what you're doing, there's no room in your concentration on the task at hand to worry or focus on other things. You can only concentrate on flying.

Then, in August, a card arrived for me in the post. It had first gone to Cambridge, to my sister. It was from Bernard. He was still alive and in a prisoner of war camp in Brunswick, Germany, Oflag 79. My sister had phoned me beforehand to tell me the amazing news. At least we could now correspond. But of course I had no idea, even when we knew the war was ending, when they'd get him home.

They'd been desperately short of food in Germany, so POWs got very little food. By the end of the war, there was no food at all in the camp. So the men were getting out of the camp and scavenging around the countryside to see what they could find.

Finally, the Americans got to the camp and released them. We heard on the BBC Home Service news on 14 April 1945 that Allied troops had reached Bernard's camp. The POWs were transported to Brussels and then flown home to an aerodrome near Horsham. Below are a few extracts from the diary Bernard kept in captivity:

We were the first tanks to land on the beaches at Arromanches les Bains. Ambushed at Villers Bocage and after 'unpleasant journeys' on foot or on railway cattle trucks, arrived at Oflag 79 at Brunswick, Germany.

21 September 1944
Molly's first letter arrived. A wonderful moment, the most exciting of my POW life.

October 1944
The RAF bombed the camp. Columns of smoke 10,000 feet high.

26 November 1944
My darling's birthday, the third time we've been apart.

12 April 1945
One word: FREEDOM. US forces entered the camp at 9.30am.

24 April 1945
Landed at Dunsfold, went to the village and phoned my darling –
what a moment! Spent first sixteen weeks POW leave in the flat at
Hamble, those were happy days!

I was still working at Hamble on 24 April when Bernard rang
to say he was back. It was a very big moment, hearing his voice
again. Yet he was so used to secrecy in all things, he wouldn't tell
me where he was! In London, still in his uniform and rather smelly,
he went to hire a car. The man said: 'Where've you been, mate? We
haven't got any petrol.'

In the end he got a train to Southampton and a taxi to Hamble.
I had great trouble stopping my landlady putting the Welcome
Home bunting out. I knew he'd hate that.

It was wonderful to see each other. He was very thin. But the
separation didn't alter our feelings about each other – or about life
in general. Oflag 79 was an enormous camp in Brunswick with
2000 officer POWs. While he was there, Bernard was able to do
four concerts for the POWs, Schubert, Mendelssohn as well as his
own compositions. We'd both had an extraordinary and eventually
lucky war. The number of divorces that went on at that time was
dreadful but we really were able to carry on from where we left off.
Which was quite wonderful.

My flat in Hamble had a Yacht Club on one side and the pub, the Bugle, on the other. We stayed on in the Hamble flat for four months while Bernard was still on POW leave. The publican was incredibly kind, he'd leave six eggs out for us, little things like that. Bernard was getting double rations then – which wasn't that much – when you've been virtually starving for eleven months it takes time to get used to food again. He'd had jaundice, contracted while he was in Italy before he was captured. And he had back problems for the rest of his life – he always put it down to sleeping on a gravestone one night in Italy.

ATA went on for a while. But by that time, there were more pilots than jobs, so when Bernard came back, I came out at once. Literally overnight.

Bernard went to London to be demobbed. His Colonel wanted to put him into a pool of officers going into the Far East.

'I don't think that would be terribly wise, sir,' was Bernard's response. Bernard told him he thought he'd be more useful in the senior training corps. So he went on to a list of lecturers for the senior training corps. Effectively, he'd left the Army. Had he been totally compliant, he'd have ended up in Japan. I think he felt he'd done his bit for King and Country at that point. He'd go back to Oxford – as organist and choir master at Queen's College, tutoring music there.

Accommodation was very hard to find just after the war. In 1946 we hired a furnished house north of Oxford, 15 miles out in Charlbury, for six months. Then in July, my brother found a house for us in Bampton. We'd realised that we could live outside Oxford. I'm not particularly academic and I thought I'd get bored around too many academics. My brother rang us on a Sunday morning after he'd seen the cottage. It was a very pretty cottage. 'You'd better get here quickly, houses round here are being requisitioned,' he told us.

It was a terrific home for us. By this time, I was heavily pregnant with my first son, Graham. So on the Monday, with the help of a loan from my brother, we bought the house. We moved in the next day. It was very nearly requisitioned. But we managed to get some white paint and paint it throughout. A month after we moved in, Graham was born. Then Peter Gregory arrived in 1948 and our youngest, Nigel, was born in 1950.

I didn't fly as a pilot again after the war. When you've been flying solidly for a period of time, you almost get it out of your system. And I think women are very good at closing one door and opening another. There was no way I was going to spend Bernard's hard earned cash on flying little Austers when I'd been paid to fly during the war – £40 a month, the first-time women got equal pay with the men, thanks to the efforts of Pauline Gower.

Living in a cottage with three little boys under four keeps you pretty occupied. Life was full on. As the boys got bigger, the house got smaller. So we eventually moved to a bigger house, Appleton Manor, 6 miles outside Oxford. Bernard loved carpentry and was very good with his hands and we all worked on the house, the boys all took on a craft, one did the tiling, the other the stonewalling.

In 1955 Bernard became a Doctor of Music. I ran a girls' club in the area for a while; we were terribly hard up then, it probably would have been more useful if I'd taken a job. But I had a family, so I concentrated on them. When my father had died his will left me shares in the business, his legacy. But I don't think it hurts anyone to be hard up at some stage in life.

In 1957, I became a Magistrate, someone had recommended me. I knew nothing about it at all, a lay magistrate sitting in judgement on their peers.

'Molly, if it doesn't work, you can always resign,' Bernard told me.

Having been very reluctant to do it, I did the maximum in term time – while the boys were at boarding school – and minimum in holiday time. If I do something, I do it wholeheartedly. [Molly became Chairman of the Bench from 1977 to 1987.] I did it for 35 years until I had to retire at 70; I'm still involved as Vice President. I found it fascinating. It made me a more tolerant person. You understand human nature much more. On the bench my colleagues came from all walks of life.

You don't enjoy the work in the accepted sense, of course. But it makes you more tolerant of people who do commit crimes. You could see why. You could see it in their backgrounds, understand why it was happening.

As for flying, over the years we flew all over Europe and America when Bernard's choir were giving organised tours in various churches and cathedrals. On one occasion, about 25 years back, I was flying in a business jet, a Cessna Citation, and the pilot offered to let me take over. We were in the right lane and the right height so I did. I didn't land it – I'd never landed a Citation before and after all, it was over 50 years after the war – but I drove it all the way back home. If there'd been a disaster, say the pilot or co pilot had a stroke, I still felt I could cope. But that wasn't likely to happen, thankfully. The basic principles are the same. It's like driving a car. Provided you know which things make things work, you'll be alright. But that was the last time I sat at the controls.

After living there for 23 years, we left Appleton Manor and came here to live in Bampton. Appleton Manor, once the boys were all married, was no house for getting old in, it was far too big. If you forgot something, it was a route march to go and fetch it – and we knew that neither of us could have gone on there alone.

I've now been in Bampton for over 25 years. We made a lot of friends here. And, of course, there's our family. Graham is now a retired PR consultant, Peter Gregory is a musical conductor and Nigel runs a security company. Between them, I have five grandchildren.

In the early 1990s, Bernard started to get ill with emphysema. He was 75. And it got progressively worse. In the last few years of his life, he became quite an invalid. Yet in a way, it was one of the happiest times of our life. We stopped being involved socially in the village. We'd ask people round for an hour or two if he felt well enough, to catch up on village gossip, that sort of thing. I was happy, looking after him here.

The last two years of his life were very special. We both enjoyed church music because it was his work (Bernard was awarded an OBE in 1980 for services to music). Vaughan Williams was a big favourite, Bernard knew him from student days. And we'd do crosswords, starting in the morning and continuing through the day; we allowed ourselves dictionaries.

Bernard died, aged 80, in November 1996. I'm fortunate in that I've got a very strong faith. It's grown with the years. And I'm happy to accept what the Almighty does for me. I am a member of Exit, everyone around me knows this. Quite recently, I decided the right thing to do was to get my grandson to engrave a 'no resus please' statement on a medallion to go around my neck. I've been laughing about it with some of my bridge playing friends.

He was horrified. 'You can't mean that,' he said. Then there was a general kerfuffle in the family about it all. But I really don't want to be any more trouble to anyone and become a cabbage. I sent a note out to all the family. Now I wear this silver chain with a little pink plastic heart – if they don't look at that, they need to be shot at dawn.

I've tried to be useful in life. After the war, one did any community work one could, a continuity of caring about people. So many women now work full-time, life has become more difficult for people, most married couples really need two incomes and that stops them from having time to help other people. Now of course, so much voluntary work is done by older people – because they've got the time.

We all knew we had our backs to the wall in the war. Without a doubt, the British are at their best in that kind of situation. There was no question of social standing or class. If anyone had a problem and you could help, you jolly well did. And, of course, whatever happened, you knew there were always people who had far worse situations to cope with.

I was never stopped from doing anything because I was a woman. And while the women of the ATA were unique as a group of civilian women pilots flying for Britain during the Second World War, they weren't the only female wartime pilots. Russian and Czech women were flying too – and they were in combat.

In my view, I had always been fortunate; first my father looked after me, then my brother, then Bernard. And now, in my old age, it is my sons. I was of that generation. How lucky can a seventh child be!

The girl on the cover of *Picture Post* in 1944: ATA 1st Officer, the late Maureen Dunlop from Buenos Aires, Argentina. Such was the impact of her image, it led to many people believing that *all* ATA ferry pilots were women!

Wartime Wedding Day, Hove, 23 December 1939; Molly and
Bernard Rose. Molly is just nineteen but already working as a
Flight Engineer in the family business.

Summer of 1942; Yvonne Wheatley (later MacDonald) in her late
husband Tom Wheatley's Renault. Tom was killed in a bombing
raid over Berlin in March 1943: they had been married for just
over a year.

Joy Lofthouse after completing her ATA training: 'Our parents were so proud when we came home in our uniforms.'

Joy Lofthouse at Hamble, 1944, getting ready for a day's work
delivering Spitfires from factories to airfields.

The ATA Operations Room at Hamble: organising each
day's schedule of plane deliveries was a complex exercise in
logistics and planning.

Hamble Ferry Pool, 1945. Bad weather often meant spending time playing cards or writing letters as the women waited to be cleared to fly.

Neil and Yvonne MacDonald in London on VJ Day. They went there by train and joined the happy crowds celebrating the end of the war. 'Everyone was going crazy in the streets.'

The Ferry pool at Hamble: the women pilots celebrate the end of the Second World War – yet their joy is tinged with sadness at the winding down of the ATA.

VE Day 1945: final ATA days. Joy Lofthouse (standing) with group of ATA flyers on a Fleet Air Arm Barracuda at Sherburn in Elmet, North Yorks.

Neil and Yvonne MacDonald on the wedding day at Darlington, Yorkshire. 'We just went and did it. I wept a few tears beforehand.'

1st Officer Mary (Wilkins) Ellis. She became known as the 'Fog Flyer' because of her ability to ferry planes safely in bad or foggy weather.

Mary (Wilkins) Ellis and a twin-engined Mitchell bomber. On one occasion, after she had delivered a Wellington, the RAF crew searched the plane – they didn't believe a girl could be the pilot.

After the war ended, Mary (Wilkins) Ellis took up rally driving in her beloved Allard and won many cups in competition.

Mary (Wilkins) Ellis in the control room at Sandown Airport on the Isle of Wight. Managing Director of the airport in 1950, she went on to run it for twenty years. She was the first female air commandant in the UK.

Mary (Wilkins) Ellis flew a Spitfire over Suffolk at the age of 90. 'It felt like the best day of my life.'

Margaret Frost, ATA 3rd Officer. She loved Spitfires so much, on one of her last Spitfire deliveries she wrote on the delivery slip: 'This is a beautiful aeroplane and should not be broken up.'

Monique Agazarian. She flew a naval Seafire at low level over
Knightsbridge in London on VE Day. She went on to a successful
career in commercial aviation after the Second World War.

Left to right: Mary Guthrie, Monique Agazarian and Sheila Garrett
with a Mark X14 Spitfire at Hamble in 1945, three of the elite group
of Spitfire Girls who played such an important role during the
Second World War.

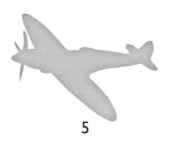

5

MARY (WILKINS) ELLIS

Mary was born in Oxfordshire in 1919. She joined the ATA on 1 October 1941, leaving on 31 December 1945 as a 1st Officer. She delivered 400 Spitfires to 210 airfields, flew 76 different types of plane and flew a total of 1000 aircraft.

At one stage during her time as an ATA pilot, Mary Wilkins was known to her colleagues as 'The Fog Flyer' because of her skill in delivering planes in atrocious weather conditions. On one memorable occasion, after delivering a heavy twin-engined Wellington bomber to an RAF station, the officers there demanded to know where the pilot was. They just couldn't comprehend that a slim, fair-haired young twenty-something woman could have piloted such a mighty war machine to its destination.

One of five children from a comfortable Oxfordshire farming family, Mary's entire adult working life has been spent in aviation. After the ATA Hamble ferry pool disbanded, she was one of three women to continue ferrying planes for the RAF for six months. Then she became a private pilot to a businessman, eventually setting up an air charter business with six aircraft. As a result, she became Europe's only woman Air Commandant, Managing Director of Sandown Airport, on the Isle of Wight, for two decades.

Reserved, graceful and still as passionate about flying as she was as a small child on her first ever joy flight in the 1920s, hers is an awesomely distinguished flying career. She retains that low-key modesty that is the hallmark of the surviving Spitfire Girls. You leave Mary (Wilkins) Ellis with the impression that this woman could cope with anything life threw at her, even in her nineties.

'I Must Have Been Born With the Instinct to Fly'

I was a very sickly child. My father, Charles Wilkins, was a farmer with 1000 acres of land on Langley Farm in Oxfordshire. It is a very historic place, a former hunting lodge for Henry VIII and an annexe to the Palace of Woodstock. I had two older brothers, one younger and one sister, Dora, eight years younger than me.

We had a cook and a housemaid and at one stage I had a nanny to look after me because I was always ill: I had pneumonia several times. Even now I can still remember my nanny, Amy, saying to me: 'Mary, you must be quiet. And stay in bed.'

It was a very happy childhood; we were a close family living on a big farm with tiny little pigs – adorable when small – and cows. My mother, Ellen, was a parson's daughter and my father came from a farming family so it was a hard working rural life, he was either out working on the farm or going to market. They were good to us, we were well looked after, all of us going off to church a mile away every Sunday.

My father owned a big American car, a Studebaker and also a Model T Ford. There weren't many cars around in those days, of course, but my lifelong fascination with cars and planes probably started from there.

By the time I was around eight, I became healthier. I've remained that way for the rest of my life. At the local school at Shipton under Wychwood, I wasn't particularly sporty but I was a very lively child, very interested in everything that was going on and I liked school. I wasn't particularly good at cooking or anything remotely domestic, however.

The desire to fly came to me at a very early age in the mid 1930s when the flying circuses were drawing the crowds. I'd have been about eleven or twelve. I remember a bright, lovely day, enhanced by the sound of aircraft – Sir Alan Cobham arriving at Witney aerodrome. My father had promised me and my three brothers that we could go to see the flying circus planes.

I was desperate to have a joy flight too and my excitement knew no bounds when I climbed into the DH 60 Moth, propped up with cushions so that I could see out of the cockpit, and off we went up into the sky. It was the most wonderful experience I'd ever known. I remember that feeling of exhilaration right to this day. I knew I simply had to do this again. I had to know how to fly. But at that point, I had no idea how I'd be able to do this. I was just a schoolgirl, after all.

We had some interesting neighbours at Langley. The Mitford children lived nearby. Their father had built a big house at Swinbrook, near Burford in the Cotswolds and as a child, if the young Mitford girls spotted me out walking, they'd offer me a ride home with them in their horse-drawn carriage. Later, of course, they would become well known. But to us then, they were just … our neighbours.

When I was around twelve we moved from Langley to the Manor House at Brize Norton. My father needed more space, a bigger area for farming. He'd also purchased another farm and put in a manager there. We found ourselves living in a much bigger building, it had been a monastery at one time. After the move, I went to school at Burford, in the Cotswolds, first to a secondary school, then to the High School where the educational standards were very high. Looking back, it was an idyllic place to grow up in.

At around the age of sixteen, because of my enthusiasm for flying, my school agreed to give me the time off to go to the aerodrome and try some flying lessons. I was the only one in the family to be fascinated by planes and flying. My brothers and sisters weren't at all interested. My father had an instinct towards aviation but he didn't learn to fly himself. Yet he was happy to pay for my lessons. Little did we know what a great adventure it would all turn out to be.

I learned to fly at the Witney airfield on the Swallow single-engine aircraft and the De Havilland 60 Gypsy Moth. As I climbed out of the plane after that exciting first lesson, I could hardly wait for the next one. It's hard to really put it all into words. I just knew I simply had to do this. I had a real enthusiasm for life itself – but this was definitely the big thing.

Of course, planes were very flimsy in the mid 1930s. And you couldn't fly whenever you wanted because of the weather, so it was difficult to even get a lesson (which cost my father about 12s 6d at the time). So it was some time before I could actually go solo and get my licence, by which time I'd left school.

In all, I did about fourteen hours' flying over a long period of time. I even got to meet other women like myself at Witney. I had two male instructors and there was one female assistant instructor from South Africa, Jackie Sorour (later to become Jackie Moggridge), studying for her commercial licence. She came with me on my first cross-country flight from Witney to Walsall. I thought it was great to see another female, the first other woman flyer I ever encountered. Jackie, of course, would also go on to join the ATA in the summer of 1940, more than a year before me. But all this was way ahead of us.

At one stage when I knew I would soon be having my first solo flight, I asked my parents to come to see me at Witney, I was so excited about it all. So they watched me, in fear and trepidation, as I had another lesson prior to my first solo flight.

As for me, I was on Cloud Nine. I was elated, there's no other way to describe it. I was very fortunate. My father happily financed my obsession. He wanted me to fly, no question.

But of course, while I was happily living at home on the farm without a care in the world, the world outside us was darkening. I'd never heard the possibility of war discussed in detail – I think my parents kept their early fears about war with Germany to themselves – but when war came in September 1939, all civil flying stopped.

My brothers were not called up because they were already at farming college, and farmers, like my father, were not called up either. But the war itself didn't mean anything to me at that stage. I'd seen my mother start crying when the news of war came over the radio. She obviously understood what it all meant. But as a young woman, still living in the sticks, I didn't; no one really knew what was going to happen.

But while I couldn't fly any more, I had a few boyfriends around me who did. Living at Brize Norton, of course, they tended to be lads in the RAF who were already flying. So being in their company helped maintain my enthusiasm for flying itself. Of course, in the strictest sense, you were not supposed to talk about what was going on a day-to-day basis during the war. But there was certainly some talk. And I could see the planes for myself, so I knew what they were flying.

By 1941, the ATA was starting to ferry aircraft from maintenance units as well as from the factories and more ferry pilots were urgently needed. One day in early autumn I was listening to the radio when I heard something that stopped me in my tracks: the authorities were keen to hear from any civilian women who had a pilot's licence to join the recently formed Air Transport Auxiliary.

I ran to my mother in the drawing room and told her: 'Oh my goodness, I've got a licence, I can apply!' She was shocked. My father wasn't quite ready for this either. 'I don't mind the flying,' he said. 'But I don't want you to go to war.'

But nothing was going to stop me. They wanted women who were qualified to fly and I had the qualification. Within days, I was called to my ATA interview at Hatfield. I went up in a Tiger Moth with an ATA instructor from their women's pool. And when I climbed out, she turned round and said: 'I know you've not been flying for some time. But you haven't forgotten very much, have you?'

We walked back to the office and she went in to see Pauline Gower. When she came out I was told: 'OK, we'll write to you.' I didn't have to wait very long for that letter. It said: 'We'd like you to join us as soon as possible.' I was in seventh heaven. But my father was adamant: no fighting.

'Oh I don't think it's fighting,' I told him. And he accepted that. So I joined the ATA women's pool at Hatfield in October 1941. I was 22. That was how it all began.

Four women pilots joined at that time. We were taken on three month's probation. I could fly a plane but, of course, I still had to be trained for the ATA. The training was excellent. It wasn't exactly flying training. If we were going to be ferrying planes later on, we had to know how to navigate. So the training was mostly navigational, always in the air.

We started out flying Moths and Magisters, Harts and Hinds and the lovely Avro Tutor. The training would enable us to fly and deliver planes without the use of radio or other aids to navigation. We relied on maps, the compass and the watch. The general idea was to be finally pronounced fit to fly all types of Class 1 planes, with the emphasis on getting the aircraft safely to its destination.

After I'd been training for about six weeks, the King's brother, Prince George, Duke of Kent, who was then a Group Captain in the RAF, came to Hatfield to talk to us. He'd come specially to see the women. It made one realise how crucial the war work was, but you never thought of yourself as being in some way important. This was wartime. We were there to do a job, just like everyone else. Sadly, less than a year later, in August 1942, he was killed in bad weather in a flying boat crash in Scotland.

My parents, of course, didn't really know much about what was going on, they were at Brize Norton and I was billeted with several other girls in Brookmans Park in Hertfordshire. This was really the first time I'd left home, though I had my own car to get around in, an old Ford.

Our billet was a big house belonging to a banker and his wife. Fortunately, we didn't have to do very much for ourselves, most billets of this type were large houses where the owners employed servants. My billet was actually a comfortable large room in a beautiful house. Essentially, we just ate and slept there. I was extremely fortunate. Yet despite my enthusiasm, I still didn't have much experience of flying.

Oh it was so exciting in those first few months, even if it was very cold in the open cockpit Tiger Moth. You needed a helmet – I had a white leather one – and an Irvin type leather flying jacket to keep you warm. They issued us with lovely leather and canvas boots, up to the knee, and, in the open cockpit, you needed goggles sometimes. It was pretty demanding, both physically and mentally. You didn't want any exercise in the evening, put it that way.

I was desperate to stay in the ATA. I knew, however, that if I made mistakes and broke a plane, I would not be fully accepted. During this time in the navigation exercises, the instructors were assessing whether you were the right type of person who could be taught to fly faster planes. Not everyone got through the course and we were all acutely aware of the possibility of failure. You just hoped like mad that you wouldn't get thrown out.

As for those that did, I don't know how they reacted but I can assure you, there wouldn't have been any tears or shows of emotion. People didn't behave that way then. I don't even know why some were failed. Our job was to supply the RAF with these machines so they could do something about the war – that was why we were so anxious to get the planes to where they should be – and never ever break or damage one.

I don't think that we thought in terms of 'winning' the war then either. It was more a case of hoping the RAF would survive. And you must remember, I was one of the youngest at that time. In one way, it was difficult to think too much about all the things that were going on around you, if you didn't read newspapers then, it was only the wireless, as we called it, that was the source of information.

But I progressed. In January 1942 my female group were posted to HQ at White Waltham, near Maidenhead to a training pool where we learned more about weather, maps and signals and had a short engineering course to complete our training. We went in every day to a classroom for a few weeks, learning more about what planes do – and what they don't do. We were also starting to fly out of White Waltham, progressing from Tiger Moths to flying planes like the Harvard.

You had an instructor for the Harvard. That training went on for a few weeks and finally you were authorised to fly Class 1 planes, the light single-engine planes – and could start the real work, ferrying the planes wherever they needed to go. I didn't feel apprehensive in any way once the initial training had ended. I thought it was incredibly exciting being a uniformed ferry pilot with my smart Austin Reed uniform. Getting the uniform was a terrific moment, it made being a pilot real somehow; complete with the gold braid.

The working day for ferry pilots began at 9.00am when you'd arrive to learn which types of plane you'd be delivering and where you'd be flying to. Then you'd go on to do the all-important weather check, study the maps and then there was the rush to get out to the taxi plane taking you to the point where you'd be starting the actual delivery. In the very early days in 1942, my deliveries were mostly Tiger Moths, Maggies, Harts and Hinds out of Luton.

People often wonder how we could fly as many as three or four different types of plane in a single day. The answer, of course, was the very thorough basic training and the wonderful little Blue Book, the Pilots Notes which had been produced by very experienced pilots in the technical section of the organisation. And your training to fly the different classes or grades of plane was progressive, depending on how well you did.

By August 1942, I was seconded to White Waltham again and learned to fly Class 2 planes, the advanced single-engined aircraft, the Hurricanes, Spitfires, Lysanders, Defiants, Mustangs and Typhoons. By October of that year, I was flying all types of single- and twin-engined aircraft from the all-women ferry pool at Hamble.

And that, of course, meant flying the Spitfire. I'd already flown Hurricanes when one morning – 13 October – I turned up to work and my chit told me I'd be ferrying a Spitfire from South Marston near Swindon, to RAF Lyneham. That was my first ever Spitfire delivery. Then, once I'd delivered the first Spit, I would be picked up by a taxi plane to take me back to South Marston, where I'd be flying the second Spitfire to the RAF at Little Rissington. On the very same day.

I'd never been close to a Spitfire before, so I was very anxious that I should do the right thing. This was a fast fighter plane. I'd better be good. Just as I was getting in, an engineer helpfully took my parachute and put it in.

'Hope you enjoy your flight, how many have you flown?' he enquired. He was horrified, poor man, when I explained it was my first Spitfire. And so the engineers moved the battery away and ground crew removed the chocks and after I'd waved them away, a group of male engineers just stood there, watching me, wanting to see what would happen as I taxied out to the take off point.

I'm sure my little heart was beating very fast but ... I was off! And somehow I managed an excellent take-off; once I was in the air, I did a few manoeuvres to make sure I knew what I was doing. And then I set off for RAF Lyneham, a 30-minute flight. Thankfully, it was a very nice day. The Spit handled beautifully. It was thrilling.

But, of course, there was the landing. As I've explained, there were no aids, you just went round the aerodrome and looked for a space between whatever else was flying and took your turn to land. I made a perfect landing. All my anxiety disappeared completely. From that day on, I fell in love with flying fast and furious aeroplanes.

As for those guys on the ground who watched me take off, I think they were horrified that this little fair haired young girl was flying a very valuable war machine twice in one day. But they seemed very happy when I got back to ferry the second one. One guy even gave me some of his sweet coupons as a reward.

I'd made a lot of friends of both sexes during my time at White Waltham while we were being trained. At Hamble, as it turned out, I made one close friend. Dora Lang, a married woman who had joined the ATA before me and at one point she was billeted in the same house at Bursledon, a few miles outside Hamble. So we could discuss things, help each other.

At the Hamble pool, you'd sometimes be sitting around, waiting for the weather to clear. Dora and I would play backgammon together. Other girls knitted or sewed. Or, if time permitted, a few of us would go to the local hospital near Hamble to visit the wounded servicemen, to try to cheer them up. We wouldn't be allowed to spend very long with them. But doing this helped everyone really.

Our commanding officer, Margot Gore, was wonderful. She knew us all, knew exactly what we could or could not do in the air. That was important. They really had to have the right person for each job.

One morning in December 1942, Dora and I turned up for work to learn that we were both delivering P1 Spitfires to the RAF Maintenance unit at Wroughton Airfield, near Swindon.

When we took off from Chattis Hill, near Southampton, the weather wasn't very good. And although it was a short flight, around 20 minutes, as we got closer to Wroughton, the weather just got worse. We'd completely lost visual contact with each other. I already knew that in this situation, I had to land as soon as possible. I also knew I was very close to the airfield at Wroughton and through the mist, I saw the shape of one of the hangars. I made a quick circuit to find the runway. I could just about see it. Then I made my approach and landing.

It was on the landing run that suddenly to my horror, something whisked past me going in the opposite direction. It was another Spitfire, it was a miracle that we had passed on the same runway at the same time. And it was Dora.

Fortunately, we had both observed the important rule of landing, by keeping to the left of the runway. And that is what saved both of us, a unique situation. As we both made our landing approach, we were in a contrary direction from the other end of the runway. We'd passed within feet of each other on the runway going in opposite directions!

Later, Dora wrote this in my autograph book: 'And the next time we land on the same aerodrome on the same runway may we both be going in the same direction!'

It wasn't my only hairy moment. One day, I was flying near Pershore, near Evesham and suddenly I saw this plane beside me. This was very unusual. I didn't want another plane close to me, I was on my course and I didn't want to lose my way. It was not a particularly clear day either. So I waved him away.

He didn't go. So I waved him again because I was going off course. Then he waved back. Then, suddenly … he was gone. I don't know what type of plane it was but it had some peculiar markings on the tail and on the fuselage. I couldn't bear to think he was German. But to this day, I don't know who he was. I was very frightened at the time. It was not a plane I thought I knew.

On another occasion, I was flying from Berkshire down South and the weather was very misty. I passed over the coast and looked out of the plane to see puffs of smoke. I realised I was being fired at. I quickly turned round and flew back inland. I must have strayed over the coast and the locals obviously thought that I was enemy aircraft. So they used the anti-aircraft battery. Fortunately, there was no damage.

Obviously, the airfields were targeted, though quite often the Germans missed. Bombing was not very accurate. But if an airfield was bombed, deliveries for that airfield were halted for a time. Throughout the war, all the RAF airfields were camouflaged and difficult to find.

Another time, I was taking off in a Spitfire from Chattis Hill when the undercarriage refused to fully retract. It was jammed in the halfway up position. I tried all sorts of maneouvres to get it to move. No luck. The best option was to land back at Chattis.

As I came down, I could see a fire engine and ambulance waiting by the side of the landing area. They knew I was in trouble, watching me making the manoeuvres and they shot off a green flare, which told me all preparations were ready for a forced landing. Which was, I suppose, a sort of comfort. I managed to make a forced landing. It was a slithery stop, which unfortunately resulted in some damage to the plane.

In May 1943, I had a week's conversion course at White Waltham authorising me to fly Class 3 planes, the light twin-engine planes. By August that year, I'd completed a two-week conversion course, authorising me to fly Class 4 planes, the advanced twin-engine Wellingtons, Hudsons, Blenheims and many other types.

I was doing well. We worked thirteen days on with two days off every fortnight and mostly, I went home then. My parents were always delighted to see me. But they didn't ask too many questions. They didn't say 'Oh Mary, are you flying Wellingtons now?' They wouldn't have known about these planes, anyway.

So in a way, I lived in two worlds, in one you got into the cockpit and flew wherever you were asked to fly, delivery after delivery so the RAF could take the planes into combat. And in the other peaceful world of the Cotswolds, everything was calm, serene, even in wartime. We had a tennis court, so I could play tennis with the local farmers' wives sometimes. It was easy to slip in and out of these two worlds.

I loved the Spitfire, like all the other pilots. But I also liked flying the twin-engined bombers, especially the Wellington. The first time I ever saw one my reaction was: 'Oh if only I could fly that.' It was ginormous. It seemed the tail was a mile away when you looked back. The RAF flew them into combat with a crew of two pilots, a navigator and an engineer. I did so love flying it alone – solo.

At one point, I had to deliver a Wellington to an RAF station, the first time a Wellington had been delivered there. After I'd landed it at the airfield, a 'follow me' car guided me to dispersal. Then, when I climbed down through the hatch with my parachute, the ground crew were there to greet me.

'Where's the pilot?' one guy said.

'I am the pilot,' I told them.

They shook their heads as if to say this couldn't possibly be true. Then one of them decided to check inside the plane. Of course, when they realised I was the pilot, they were incredulous. In combat, they needed five men inside the Wellington. But to deliver, it took just one young woman.

On another occasion, as I stepped out of a plane I'd just delivered, the airfield's Commanding Officer was watching from the tower. When he saw me, he was heard to ask who was responsible for teaching the ATA girls to fly all the different types of planes. I never saw the expression on his face. But I can imagine what it was like when he was told: 'Nobody, sir. They learn from their little Blue Book.' Referring, of course, to the ATA Pilots Notes.

That incident with the Wellington was, really, the only example of what they'd call sex discrimination nowadays. We were all too busy with our work to question who did what. A handful of girls had already shown they were capable of doing this job in the early years of the war. Now, there were more of us, simply because they needed more pilots. And we could do it.

That, of course, was largely due to the work of one woman, Pauline Gower.

I'd see her briefly sometimes and we'd have a short chat, though there were never any long, detailed conversations. She was fantastic, so interested in what all the women were doing and how we could do it. On one occasion she said to me: 'Oh you're doing very well, Mary.' That was a great compliment.

On the social side, being based on the south coast where there was so much activity, especially in 1944 and the run up to D-Day, I had a number of wonderful boyfriends, platonic. I was totally absorbed by the flying, though, so my focus was very much on my work.

My boyfriends tended to be soldiers stationed briefly around the coast. Occasionally we'd have a little dance at the club house at Hamble and we'd invite them to that. Then they'd disappear.

On one occasion, I'd had engine failure while flying a Fairchild Argus over the New Forest. So I had to force land quickly. The only open space was to the rear of the Balmer Lawn Hotel, which at the time was taken over by Marines. I managed to land safely but just as I landed, a herd of cows came galloping up. That did scare me. Luckily, a Marine spotted me and ran over to 'rescue' me. After that, I had several boyfriends from the Marines. They were all keen to take out an ATA girl in her nice smart uniform. So if the weather was bad, they'd offer to take you out for lunch. Or dinner.

Yet those were the brighter times: the downside was that very few of us came through the war without experiencing loss. In my family, we were lucky, there were no losses. But at work, it was different. One morning in early March 1944, I reported for work at Hamble as usual only to be taken aside.

There'd been an accident in a Mosquito flying out of Lasham, in Hampshire involving two girls. One was flying, the other was a flight engineer, Janice Harrington, to whom she'd been giving a lift. They were coming into land when something went horribly wrong. Instead of landing, the plane shot into the air, came down too fast on the runway and burst into flames. Both girls were dead. The pilot was my friend Dora Lang.

It was a very bitter blow. My CO said 'Mary, you won't be flying for a few days. Come to the airfield. But don't fly.'

I went to the airfield. And after two days I was allowed to fly again. I didn't talk to anyone about it. It was just too sad. Every day, we knew this was a reality. But at the same time, we never expected anything to happen. You knew the danger but you kept it right at the back of your mind. If you didn't concentrate completely on what you were doing in the air, you'd be the danger. Yes, others like me found themselves in exactly the same situation when someone they knew well died. But we never really talked about it.

Nowadays people have a cold – which is nothing much in the general scheme of things – and you find they go on and on about how dreadful it is. That's how it is today. People tell everyone everything. Back then, you never talked about things. And I'm still like that. My generation was so different to younger people now. We didn't see the need to talk about everything in our lives all the time, partly because of consideration for others. And because we had been raised that way. Perhaps the difference between then and now for us was also because aviation itself was so different for us back then. As soon as you got into the plane, no one could think for you, or tell you anything. You were alone. As long as you knew what you were doing, there was no fear. For some reason, you were always very confident. When you get great fear, that's when the danger comes in, isn't that the case?

Today in flying it's more important to be able to talk to someone on the ground than it is to actually fly. That's not my idea of aviation. You can't go anywhere unless you are talking to someone and asking them, where can I go? Yet we were trained properly to think for ourselves. Time was short, so we had to be taught well.

Not a single thing was taught that was not necessary – simply because there was so much to think about. And, of course, we could not talk openly about these things that we were doing during the war. We couldn't say where we'd been, where we were going: it was *all* secret. That might be one of the reasons why people like us haven't said anything about what we did for all those years. We were a generation who were trained to keep quiet.

Of course, you could discuss some things with other people in the ATA but when we went out to the pub, as we did occasionally, we couldn't say anything to anyone else because you never knew, someone might be listening. It's virtually impossible to think that way nowadays.

In April 1944, I was sent off for a ten-day training course on the Hudson. And in May that year, my logbook records delivery after delivery: 25 planes in one month, sometimes you'd be delivering up to four planes in a single day. We were, of course, steadily getting closer and closer to D-Day, the real turning point in the war.

My memory of that time was watching the gradual build-up for the invasion from the air. About two weeks before 6 June, four of us from ATA were flying over the Solent in a taxi plane. We could see all the landing craft there, waiting. Then one girl – I don't remember who – had a bright idea. Since there were going to be lots of men around the landing craft, why didn't we try putting a message in a bottle, with our names and where we could be found?

That way, some handsome chap would pick up the message and come and find us. How stupid we were! We laughed and threw the bottles out of the air taxi, as close to the landing craft as we could. But of course, it was really a silly distraction for us, a release from tension, if you like.

By 5 June, the Solent was full of ships. You couldn't see the water. The roads were full of tanks, the most amazing sight. Virtually every surface was covered. And then, on the 6th, they'd all gone. Everything had disappeared, as if by magic. Only it wasn't magic, of course. It was a very successful landing.

The message in a bottle incident wasn't my only attempt to communicate my existence to a handsome warrior. On 15 September, I had to deliver a brand-new Mark 8 Spitfire from Eastleigh, near Southampton, to RAF Brize Norton in Oxfordshire. Whilst I was waiting for the taxi plane to come and collect me, I decided to leave my mark, yet again. So I wrote my name in pencil 'F.O. Mary Wilkins, ATA' on the inside of the cockpit in the hope that some handsome RAF fighter pilot would see it. And my message would, in time, be discovered. But not quite in the way I'd hoped ...

By the time VE Day came, of course, I had mixed feelings. The war was ending but there I was, doing work I thoroughly enjoyed. I'd made wonderful friends and I'd wound up flying military aircraft at 500 miles an hour, something I'd never dreamed of. My family too, the hub of my existence, after all, had been very good about what I was doing, very gracious. But soon we wouldn't be needed any more. So what was I going to do? I couldn't come up with any answers.

One of the things that was really sad about the end of it all was having to fly planes to a location where they'd be scrapped. You'd be thinking 'this is terrible' but, of course, it was cheaper to scrap some of them than keep them. They'd become superfluous to the supply that was needed. One day I was flying a Whitley bomber to be scrapped and when I got to my destination I asked: 'what can I take before you scrap it?'

I was told the only thing I could take was the loo (which looked like an oil drum). I didn't want the loo. But these old bombers all carried a small axe, kept in case the pilot had to chop their way out of the plane if there was an accident. So I asked if I could please have the axe. I accepted it gratefully. And I've still got it!

In August 1945 when Hamble was due to close and the ATA disbanded, I was told I'd be seconded to White Waltham, one of three women who would be needed to continue to ferry planes for the RAF. There I was able to fly Meteor twin jet fighters, which was quite an incredible experience. I'd never seen one before, this was an entirely different type of plane.

My last Great Flight started when I was taken by air taxi from White Waltham to Moreton Valance in Gloucester, where they made these machines: the Meteor was large, so different, no propellers. I asked the test pilot if he could tell me anything about the plane's flying characteristics. He said the thing to watch was the fuel consumption. 'The fuel gauge goes from full to empty in 35 minutes,' he warned me, 'so you had better be on the ground in 30 minutes. And when you prepare to land, the power will mean that the aircraft will drop like a stone.'

That was it. After reading the notes, off I went, my destination 222 Squadron at Exeter. It was exhilarating. I was concentrating so hard on my landing, I didn't realise until I looked down that a whole crowd of people had actually gathered around the control tower.

I landed quite safely, taxied up to dispersal close to the control tower and got out. I was amazed to see a bunch of RAF officers standing in the crowd. They couldn't believe that this little girl had delivered their new plane to them. They were changing over then, from Spitfires to Meteors – and this was the first Meteor the RAF pilots were due to fly. I had no idea where it was heading;

we were never given that sort of information. But the CO there thought it was all marvellous. In fact, we corresponded for some time afterwards. It was all quite innocent, very much an aviation friendship!

In March 1946, I ferried my last ever Spitfire from Eastleigh to Culham, Oxfordshire. My work as a ferry pilot for ATA was over. Now I'd be going back to Brize Norton where nothing much had changed.

I went home and started writing off for a few flying jobs. But of course, there was nothing. All the other girls had been saying 'It's the end of us ever flying' but I couldn't give up hope that I could find something. I liked farm life, I was quite happy to be on the farm. And my passion for flying also meant a passion for fast cars. So I bought an Allard, the first new car that came out after the war, and I was able to take it rally driving. I won rally driving cups. But my dream of flying again never deserted me. My father understood this somehow. And he'd even mentioned it to a few friends. Through a friend of a friend of his, three years later, I finally landed an interview – on the Isle of Wight.

John Stephenson-Clarke was a London businessman who owned two farms, one on the island and the other near Gatwick in Surrey. He was moving around to and from the farms on weekends. And he wanted another mode of transport to get him around. It had been suggested to him that he could fly between the two.

Would I be interested in ferrying him around? He'd bought a single-engine Proctor, a four-seater. At the time, the plane was kept at Cowes airfield on the Isle of Wight, in order to fly from Cowes to Gatwick. But later he made a landing area on his farm on the island, near Newport and another landing area in Sussex. And the Proctor was swapped for a twin-engine plane, a Gemini.

So in 1949, I was back in the flying world after a long delay. I moved to the island then. I didn't particularly want to come to the island – I hate water – and in a way, it was an unusual place to come to. But I came because of the job. It meant I could fly and that was what really mattered.

I knew I was incredibly fortunate, an ex-ATA girl still working as a private pilot after the war. Later, my boss acquired Sandown Airport, which wasn't very big at the time – it was just a small flying club type place – but over time I helped him develop it. Sandown Airport hadn't been used in the war but gradually, I managed to get all the operations going. You had to make sure you had all the facilities that were needed by an airline at an airport – eventually we had Customs there too.

By 1950 I became Managing Director of Sandown Airport, the first female airport commandant in the UK. I also became Managing Director of Bees Flight Limited, a charter company with three planes. I was even able to employ another girl from ATA, my friend Vera Strodl, as a flying instructor. By 1951, the business was thriving. We were running a charter company flying business people to and from the mainland. We also had flights for holidaymakers coming in from places like Croydon, Leeds, Birmingham, London, Bournemouth and Manchester on weekends and on busy days Vera would be taking people up around the island on pleasure flights.

I subsequently ran Sandown Airport for 20 years. By the early 1960s, it was a thriving business with commercial planes coming in from all over the UK during the years when English seaside resorts were still very popular.

Each year, I'd have to hire commercial pilots for the pleasure trips. And one day, a handsome, intelligent and charming man turned up for a job. His name was Donald Ellis. He'd been in the Fleet Air Arm and had gone to Canada for training towards the end of the war. By the time he arrived back in England, the war had ended. I hired him and everyone loved him. And there was no reason why I shouldn't too.

For years, people would ask me why I wasn't married. But I was so busy with the planes, I didn't have time for romance. In a way, I was married to the planes. Donald was younger than me – but we were very happy together.

We were married at a little Church at Swinbrook, near Burford in the Cotswolds. Just after we married, something happened that was so astonishing, it made me wonder about fate – and where it can lead us.

Donald had decided to buy a plane. It was a BA Swallow, a single-engine plane, a two-seater with an open cockpit. When he eventually showed it to me, I stood there in shock. I simply couldn't believe it; because this was the very same plane I had learned to fly on in Witney all those years before. During the war it had been housed somewhere. Now it was Donald's. He had many friends and he bought a hangar on the airfield to house it, so he could take his friends flying. In the end, I didn't go in it many times. But I believe that plane is still flying today. It's nearly 80 years old.

Once we were married, I continued to run the airfield. In the years before we'd married, I'd also acquired a small boutique in Ryde, selling expensive dresses. It was called 'Lady Katie' (after TV personality Katie Boyle who was very popular at the time). I had a manageress running it but after Donald and I married, I sold it.

Then Donald was headhunted to work for British Hovercraft. And so we made a permanent home here on the island, in the house I still live in. Originally, it was an isolation hospital. We knocked it down and had a new house built, living on site in a caravan while it was being completed.

Then people's habits changed. Holidaymakers were now looking to fly abroad for their good times. So I gave up my position at the airfield and it was eventually sold.

In 1970, Donald was posted by British Hovercraft to the Middle East. By then, he was demonstrating the hovercraft all over the world, teaching people how to operate it. I would have been happy to stay put. But Donald was most anxious that I be with him at all times. So I went with him.

We lived abroad for four years. For me, there was nothing terribly exciting about it. Donald's position was high enough that we were frequently entertained at the British Embassy. And the only good thing with the deal was that every three months, we went somewhere else, Italy, Egypt, France, Spain, Bahrain, you had to have a break from the place. It was so hot. And there was nothing for a woman to do. No roads, no phones, nothing.

We did have a very nice house in Jeddah, next door to the Australian Air Attaché. But the houses had a ten-foot wall around them so we didn't even see our neighbours unless we arranged to play golf with them in the desert. But you had to do that at 5.00am – because of the heat. I learned how to play golf. But, of course, as a woman, you could never go out anywhere alone. For someone who adores driving and flying it was like hell.

We got back to the island in 1974. Donald was still working with British Hovercraft but after a while he was offered the position of airport manager at Sandown Airport by the new owner. After being abroad for four years, I was that much older and less interested in flying, keen on leading a more normal life. I think the fact of not being able to fly for those years 'cured' me of the desire to fly all the time. To get back into it is quite difficult after a gap of four years. You need to be in practice to fly. It's not easy to pick up again when you've been away from it for some time.

What was really sad was that while we were away, both my parents, then in their eighties, died within a year of each other. Over time, my brothers passed on too. Now I have one widowed sister, Dora Brown, who lives in Romsey, Hampshire.

In 1978 I was very proud when Donald was awarded the OBE for his work with the British Hovercraft Corporation and I was able to accompany him to Buckingham Palace to receive it.

Donald didn't retire. He managed the airfield, then he bought a four-seater Cessna 172 for pleasure flying rides. He did the flying and I sold the tickets – or talked the tourists into flying. After all, to me flying is something everyone has to do.

In January 1980, a vintage warbird man, Robs Lamplough, got in touch with us. He told us he had just imported a Spitfire MV 154 from Australia. The plane had been assembled in 1960 in Australia but never flown as the then owner could not get permission to fly it. Instead he had suspended it from the roof in his hangar and there it had remained, unopened and untouched for two decades.

When the owner died, Robs was able to buy the aircraft from the deceased estate. Imagine his amazement upon getting the plane back in the UK, opening the cockpit to find ... my name written in the cockpit!

According to the plane's logbook I'd flown that Spitfire for 25 minutes – and it turned out I had been the only person to fly it. You were often the test pilot when you made the delivery. And for some reason, after delivery in September 1944, the plane had gone around the different war zones. It wound up in Australia in November 1944, still in its crate from being shipped from England.

As it turned out, Robs had a few problems getting it back here because the Australian authorities said it was part of their heritage and could they please have it back? But it remained here, after all, and after a great deal of work and a replacement Merlin engine, it flew again in the summer of 1992. Of course, we went to see it and the story of me writing my name, hoping to find my handsome Air Force pilot, caused much laughter with Robs and his family. Because in the end, I did find him.

In 2007 Donald was 82 and we got the bad news that he had leukaemia. It was a rather nasty kind of leukaemia – very few people get it – and he gradually faded away over a period of eighteen months. He was in hospital and then he was in a local nursing home. It was a very sad time for me. But it's something we can't get away from. We all have to bear this. The person's death comes as a nasty shock – even though you think you are expecting it.

I still see Joy Lofthouse and Molly Rose at ATA reunions. I kept in touch with a lot of the other ATA girls but, one by one, they've gone now. There was an ATA girl living here on the island, Bennie Willis. We'd often go out for lunch. But now she's gone too.

The ATA years, when I look back, were the best time of my life. At an ATA reunion at Maidenhead recently, I found myself sitting next to Prince Michael of Kent, one of the Queen's cousins. I asked him about flying. He told me: 'I don't fly alone, I only go with instructors.' I told him: 'I started my flying career meeting the Duke of York and now I've ended it talking to Prince Michael.'

I don't know how true it is but people joke that I'm the oldest Spitfire pilot in the world. A few years ago it was arranged by Spitfire pilot Caroline Grace that I would accompany her on a short flight in the Suffolk area. It was being filmed. At one point I took the controls of the Spit for 20 minutes. How did I feel? I was grateful to Caroline for the opportunity and I would say I felt terribly elated.

In one way, it felt like the best day of my life – the years just rolled away!

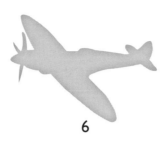

6

MARGARET FROST

Margaret was born in Sussex on 26 November 1920. She died on 4 August 2014, aged 93. She joined the ATA on 25 November 1942, leaving on 30 September 1945 as a 3rd Officer. She flew twenty-five different types of plane.

Margaret Frost was so determined to learn to fly, she overcame obstacles many other young women would have found insuperable. As an eleven-year-old she would carefully save up her pocket money just to be able to pay for the briefest of joyrides. When the Civil Air Guard was being set up just before war broke out, she was able to have some subsidised flying lessons. With war, all civil flying stopped. Still determined to fly, she applied to join the ATA women's ferry pool but was initially turned down. So she joined the WRNS.

As the need for female ferry pilots increased, she tried the ATA again – only to be told she wasn't quite tall enough. Impressed by her pluck and obvious determination, the authorities relented. Even then, there were further hurdles: her training had to be curtailed for several months because of health problems. Undaunted, she triumphantly finished her ATA training on a Spitfire and became a ferry pilot.

After the war, she worked in London as a civil servant for many years and retired to Wales in the 1970s. Softly spoken and courteous to a fault, meeting her made it clear that she was just as determined and strong-minded as she had been during those war years – a young girl who overcame all the obstacles – because she simply wouldn't give up her dream of flying.

'This is a Beautiful Plane and Should not be Broken Up'

My earliest memory of my childhood is lying in a pram on a very hot day outside the rectory at Pulborough in Sussex. I was born in Kingston Bewsey, a tiny little village in Sussex near Shoreham and Portslade. My father, Ernest Isaac Frost, was a country parson. I was born in the old rectory at Kingston, the first child to be born there for 50 years. It's still there. We moved shortly afterwards to Pulborough Rectory, a big, old, rambling rectory with a large garden.

My father had private means. He worked very hard at the Rectory. There were just two of us children, me and my brother Ernest Julian. We always called him 'Bobby'. That came from when he was very small and couldn't say the word 'baby', calling himself 'babby'. And he ended up being called Bobby all his life. There was a big age gap between us: he was over eight years older than me.

Mine was a happy childhood. But it was lonely because Bobby was so much older and away at boarding school. The gap was such that we wouldn't be playing together, anyway. My mother, Olive Jessie Thornton (as she was before she married my father), was a very kind woman. Of course, in those days you got help around the house, so the local country girls would come to help in the house as maids. We had a cook, a parlour maid called Phyllis and a housemaid. At one stage, I can remember a parlour maid called Dorothy who was very grand. She'd hand the macaroni round and pronounce it Mar-car-oni, quite a character, really. In the tradition of those days, we'd have prayers at home every morning – and all the servants attended.

I wasn't a big doll person. I do recall a ragdoll – children always have something they take to bed – but eventually they took it away from me, though I don't know why. Because of my father's role in the community, people from the village would often be coming to the house for tea. And my father was also frequently going to meetings in the village hall.

I didn't go to the local school. I had a governess from the age of about five, a woman who lived in the village. She was quite strict. I had a friend in the village, Winsome. She came and did lessons with me, but there weren't any other children my age around me. At one stage, when I was about six, my father had a curate for a while, a family of missionaries who had been in China. And they had small children I could play with. But then they went off when the curate got a parish of his own.

By the time I was nine, I had a pony and a rabbit. We also had a car. Rectors, of course, succeed each other and the rector before my father had a car, which my father then took on. It was ghastly. It was old and I can remember very cold, dark winter's evenings when the thing would get stuck because the lights would go. Or something else would go wrong. So we'd have to sit there in the cold while the groom tinkered with it.

I was aware that other children had brothers and sisters and that I was a bit isolated, so I started to badger my father about sending me to boarding school. At first, they seemed to think I was too young, but by the time I was eight and a half, they arranged for me to go to boarding school in Bognor Regis, Sussex. I wasn't happy at first. But what small child is until they settle down?

The younger children like me had to sleep right at the very top of the building – which was extremely cold – but it was a very well run and comfortable school and I made friends quite quickly with one or two girls. I am still in touch with them to this day.

I became friendly with a girl called Desirée. Her family had been living in Australia and had returned to England. We also had two

Egyptian girls there and a son of the Maharajah of Jaipur. He would arrive for school in a very grand car: he was known as 'Bubbles'. His older sister attended the school too.

There were other wealthy girls there: the daughters of J. Arthur Rank, the owner of the big cinema chain attended the school, one daughter, Pat, was very good on horseback. Bognor, to me, was just lots of little houses. So it was lovely to go back home to the countryside when school term ended.

I was about ten when something happened that set the course of what would eventually take place. One day, my mother and a couple of women friends – they were widowed women who lived in our village – decided to go on an outing by car. They were heading for a tiny airfield at Shoreham. This was because one of my mother's friends wanted to try the latest thing called flying.

My mother was the sort of person who was very good at trying things for the first time. I can remember childhood stories about her roller skating on the promenade at Southsea. But because flying was so new and people saw it as 'dangerous', they had decided to take me with them in the car, in case I went and told my father what they were doing. Rather than have him worry about it all, they decided to go off and try it for themselves; but keep quiet about it.

When we got to the little airfield we were taken to the plane. It was a Pussmoth and it turned out there was a spare seat for me. Until then, I'd enjoyed riding. I'd also learned to row a boat when I was about six – we had a large pond at the rectory – but this was something totally different. But they wouldn't let me go up with them!

I was very cross, you know how children can be. And yet as I watched them going up in the air, I knew, beyond a doubt that, no matter what, I simply had to try this marvellous new thing myself.

From that day on, I nagged everyone to let me go up in a plane. If someone said, 'What do you want for Christmas, Baby?' or

'What would you like for your birthday?' my response was always the same. 'I want to go up in a plane.' ('Baby' was my childhood nickname; only when I was thirteen did they start calling me by my full name.)

Finally, at age eleven, I got my wish; they paid for me to have a short flight. At Shoreham airfield I went up in a De Havilland Moth. That type of plane had a passenger cabin but the pilot was seated at the rear, so he could look through while seated at the controls.

The flight was all too brief for an excited eleven-year-old girl. I thought the pilot was very mean. He had spotted me moving from side to side in the cabin. I so wanted to see everything, take it all in. But I think he thought that meant I was scared: it seemed as if we were hardly up in the air at all. There was low cloud around so it was a bit bumpy. But when we got down, I climbed out, rushed over to my mother who was waiting for me and said: 'I want to go up again.' She was horrified.

From then on, I saved every penny of my pocket money or birthday money to pay to go up again myself. The Chief Flying Instructor at Shoreham at the time was Cecil Pashley, an early aviation pioneer who had started flying in 1908 and eventually wound up training large numbers of pilots in the Second World War. [One of Cecil's early pupils was aircraft designer and manufacturer F.G. Miles.] This time, he was at the controls of my flight. So I promptly asked him if he could do an aerobatic manoeuvre, a loop – something I thought was very overrated and still do, to this day. People make a great fuss about looping or 'loop the loop' (where the pilot dives down, pulls the nose up once there's enough speed and comes down the other way) but unimpressed as I was, I knew I was going to learn to fly somehow, there was no doubt in my mind.

There were huge obstacles. I didn't have any money and flying lessons were expensive. I was still at school and, of course, I was a girl. Had I been a boy then my family might have stumped up for lessons for me. But my father was, after all, a country parson, and they were not very keen on the idea of their daughter learning to fly. In those days, girls like me were supposed to remain quietly at home, or take the parish magazines around the village. It was all quite a different world then.

I got my school certificate at fifteen but I didn't matriculate – I hadn't done Latin and geometry. I'd already asked to leave if I passed school cert. But no one thought I'd manage to pass. Yet I did. In the end, I went back to school for German and French lessons a couple of days a week.

By now, it looked like war was definitely coming. As a country, we had disarmed to an extent and it quickly became obvious that we had to build up our Armed Services, particularly the Royal Air Force and the Fleet Air Arm. So the Civil Air Guard was being set up. The news was on the radio and in the papers. Then I discovered that flying clubs were going to be allowed to give flying lessons at half the usual price. The discount was being subsidised by the Government. And because Shoreham had an association with Brooklands, a large flying club, they rented a small landing ground belonging to Parham House, near Pulborough, about 5 miles from where I lived. People like me could now just about afford to have flying lessons.

When I went to ask my father if I could have the subsidised lessons he was adamant: 'No, you can't do it.' Crestfallen, I decided to say no more. Maybe he'd change his mind, I thought.

I was right. I heard him answering the phone one morning not long afterwards and heard him say: 'Oh no, there's no question of her doing it.' My hopes were squashed again. But then, a bit later on, I heard him on the phone again saying 'Nothing's been decided.' Then, later that day, I heard my father talking to someone on the phone again and saying: 'Oh, we're delighted she's doing it.'

Somehow, he'd relented because word had got round the village and people were ringing to congratulate him on the news. I suppose he was swayed by local opinion – they all saw flying lessons as a good thing!

Even then, I was stuck. You had to be eighteen to be eligible for the subsidised lessons. And my eighteenth birthday wasn't until November 1938. So all I could do was wait till then. Yet even once I'd turned eighteen, more frustration: there was no vacancy for lessons at Parham.

Only six months on, in April 1939, did I get in for my lessons. And that was because the only girl in the area who was learning to fly got engaged and promptly stopped her lessons. I started my flying lessons straight away. I'd carefully saved up all the money I could to buy goggles and a helmet. But because war was now imminent, the better flying times for the lessons earlier in the day were all allocated to the men, who were a priority.

My lesson was usually in the afternoon, which meant waiting around because the wind tended to come up around lunch time and dropped after 2.00pm. Once or twice I had to wait a fortnight between lessons. But I managed to go solo and got my 'A' licence. They started you off quite simply. I wasn't very quick going solo: I went solo after about ten hours' flying, which was average in those days, flying in the Gypsy Moth every time. For some reason, I don't know why, you don't really quite take in the moment of your first solo. The instructor just stepped out of the plane in the middle of the field and said, without any warning at all, 'OK, off you go.' I was so surprised, I just did it. Nowadays, of course, it's a tremendous business getting your 'A' licence. But then you had to get up to 2000ft, close the throttle and do a dead stick landing.

That Friday before war was declared, I went to Parham as usual, hoping for my lesson. But everyone had disappeared. No one had even come down there from Brooklands. Most of the men were reservists, anyway. I didn't really know anyone there, I just went there, had my lesson and went home again. But it was quite obvious what was happening. I didn't even attempt to contact anyone, ask questions. There would be no more lessons. Civil flying was ending.

The rectory we lived in was a big, rambling sort of place. So that same day I returned home, somewhat crestfallen, to find that evacuees had already turned up from London. A school from South East London with children ages 8–14 had been evacuated to our village, mistresses and all. My parents were housing ten children. Then two of them got homesick, so we wound up looking after eight children at the rectory through the war.

That Sunday, we all trooped off to church as usual. My father was preaching and he had organised a loudspeaker so everyone in the packed church could listen to that 11.00am broadcast from Mr Chamberlain.

As soon as the broadcast ended, we could hear a siren going off. 'Here we go,' I thought, just like everyone else. But of course, it turned out to be a false alarm, the start of the 'phoney war' months. None of us had any idea what to expect at all. Everyone thought exactly the same thing: 'OK, now we know we're at war but what is going to happen?'

For several months, I remained at home, helping out, mostly peeling potatoes in the kitchen. We still had some help in the house. One of the girls working in the house went to the WAAFs, Cook went into the WRNS, only her sister was left with us, helping to organise the evacuees.

The house had two sets of stairs, front and back, so there was plenty of room to accommodate everyone. But I often wonder how my mother managed to cope with it all. I can still remember the first thing she did that September was to buy the children mackintoshes and gumboots – after she'd ensured they'd all had a bath and their hair washed. They got our big bathroom, such as it was, and we used the tiny one. Their education continued as normal. They had their lessons, as usual, in the village hall on the following Monday after war was declared.

As the months passed at home, I knew I wanted to get involved with some sort of war work. I can even now vividly remember riding my bike, after hearing the news that yet another country had been invaded by the Germans. That time, in May 1940, it was Holland. You couldn't help it. Your thoughts were: will they invade us? How brave will we have to be? The threat of invasion was very, very real.

My chance to get involved came a couple of months later. A friend of mine in the village asked me if I'd come with her on the bus into Brighton. She wanted to pay a visit to the Recruiting Centre for the Women's Royal Naval Service 'Join the Wrens, free a man for the fleet,' was the recruitment slogan. So I went along. In the end, my friend decided not to join. But I did.

Back at home, my brother Bobby had gone into the army and my parents were more concerned about him than about me joining the WRNS. So off I went for my training at Portsmouth. They were training us in a former maternity home. On the way there, as I was changing trains, I got chatting to a girl called Joan, also heading for the same place, hoping to become a Wren. We've remained friends ever since.

Arriving at Portsmouth that day was a big shock. We'd just missed the very heavy bombing there. All around us were jagged houses, sides of homes, acres of bombed-out buildings. Here was the reality of wartime and the Blitz. It was indeed a sobering reminder of what was really happening to us.

As it worked out, most people were coming into the WRNS to be cooks. We had a fortnight's training, not much marching, scrubbing out. One day Joan and I admired the 1st Officer's dog. We were promptly asked to walk the dog daily.

After training, Joan went into motor transport. She was already an experienced ambulance driver, whereas I had only driven my father's old Humber and failed my WRNS driving test. But there was plenty of other work. I kept stores, made tea with a small kettle over a Bunsen burner and, after ten months at Portsmouth, I was transferred to different work as a 'plotter', we plotted the paths of ships in and out of their harbours. I worked out of a small plotting station and there weren't many of us doing the plotting. We worked in shifts. And you had to be very quick when it got really busy.

I was enjoying my work. But then, completely out of the blue, there was a letter waiting for me from the ATA. Would I contact them please?

In fact, I had already applied to them because right at the beginning of war, they had asked for anyone who had a pilot's licence to get in touch. I had an 'A' licence. I'd done fifteen hours in the air – with just over five hours solo. But they'd written back to me and said: 'Very sorry, no use, join something else.'

Now, of course, everything had changed. By 1942, they urgently needed more ferry pilots so my original application hadn't been in vain, at all. I had high hopes I got myself up to Maidenhead to White Waltham for the interview. I had the medical tests, eye tests and an interview with the Chief Flying Instructor who commented that I was too short. He was right. I was under height for the WRNS too. The requirement was 5ft 4in (1.62cm) or over and I am just under 5ft 3in. It looked like I wasn't going to make it. All my hopes of flying were dashed. Again.

'If that's it, I'd better go,' I said, getting up to leave.

Then, to my surprise, I was asked to sit down. He was going to discuss my application with Pauline Gower, whom I never actually met, and after that, they would be letting me know. 'In the meantime, try and grow a little,' was his parting shot.

That cheered me up no end. I knew he wouldn't have said that if they didn't want to take me. And sure enough, not long afterwards I got the letter saying they'd accept me.

I told my officer in charge at the WRNS and she then made a formal application for me to leave. In those days, anyone who had touched a plane was released because by then, they were so short of ferry pilots. I was sorry to leave because I had enjoyed my fourteen months working at the WRNS. But I'd had a letter from the ATA saying they'd take me! I'd be fulfilling my lifelong dream to fly – and doing my bit for the war effort.

It was still a very big step, despite all my enthusiasm for flying. I discussed it all with a friend. She said: 'Look, you've always wanted to do it. And if you don't do it and regret it, we'll all have to listen to you.' She was right. It would have been awful to have missed the chance and regretted it later.

So I swapped forces. The WRNS gave me a fortnight's leave before I joined the ATA and I went home to my family at Pulborough. They were busy with the war, questioning whether I should be doing this didn't come up. In fact, I never asked my parents if I could join the ATA. I just did it. My brother was in the Eighth Army so we were all thinking about him more than anything else.

And so the cold, dark November day dawned in 1942 when I took a train to my new billet in Luton, 22 Fountain Road, a very pleasant family with two small children. We had a billeting officer who organised all our billets while we were in training. And so I was ready to start my training from scratch. Some of us who were training had flown before, but they started me off this way because I had not done very much flying.

We went for our flight training to what had been a pre-war flying school at Barton in the Clay, north of the Chilterns. There were quite a lot of us. Freydis Sharland (or Freydis Leaf as she was then) and I were the only two civilian trainees, the rest were RAF people who had been seconded to the ATA by then.

Freydis and I were friends right from the word go, the only women training to be ferry pilots out of our group. Like me,

Freydis was passionate about flying. And we shared the same sense of humour. But the training was hard work. You had to think carefully about every single thing you were doing and hope that you would get it right.

But I had problems with my eyes at first. My general flying was OK, but landing wasn't easy for me. I was told by the Chief Medical Officer, 'Your eyes are terrible, how did you ever get in?'

Later I learned that in fact, they'd been lenient with me. I was under height, had little experience and it was obvious that I had lazy eyes. They still took me in nevertheless. I wound up going to see a specialist in London who said I couldn't have corrective glasses: but she prescribed two and a half months of eye exercise. I wouldn't be able to fly in that time, but I could hang around the airfield, watching everyone else. People did feel a bit sorry for me but there was a general feeling they were going to get me through. And after that time, I was ok to fly.

I was sent to the training unit at a village near Thame, Oxfordshire and an aerodrome where we were trained on the Hawker Hart, a biplane with two cockpits which was quite powerful (the original was called the Hawker Fury, a single-seater). We also flew a Fairchild Argus, a four-seater high wing monoplane, often used for collecting people, an air taxi, but we trained on this. And after this I was sent off to the ferry pool at Hamble for three weeks to get to know more about flying in the countryside, then to the other women's pool at Cosford, to get more experience flying the Fairchild. Then I returned to training at Thame, moving on to the Class 1 aircraft, the Tiger Moth, Gladiator and Swordfish – an enormous, heavy aircraft but quite easy to fly. And the Fairy Swordfish, that plane that did wonderful things in Italy.

Around Christmas time I was put forward to learn to fly the Class 2 single-engined fighters. First of all, you trained on the Harvard, very noisy with a tremendous whine for anyone who was outside the plane. The undercarriage was fairly low. And when you landed there was a great rattling noise. But it was a very kind plane. It didn't do anything horrid.

I had just soloed on the Harvard when disaster struck: I got appendicitis. I had to go off for two and a half months. While I was having my appendix out, all the women in my training group went on to the next stage. But I lost my course. Initially, I had been sent home by the medical officer with suspected blood poisoning but in fact, it was a grumbling appendix. And it had to come out immediately. I had the operation at a nursing home in Worthing, Sussex.

Pulborough was a restricted area then and you needed permission to go in and out. The nursing home was right on the seafront. The Germans would do hit and run raids so you'd hear the air raid sirens wailing all the time. I was there for ten days.

In that time, my father had had a massive heart attack at home. A friend from the village came to keep me company. When I did get home, things weren't good: my father remained poorly for several months. There was also a lot of worry about my brother Bobby in North Africa. And, of course, the appendicitis had slowed me down a lot.

It took time, but I finally returned to Thame to restart my course. To cheer me up, I was allowed to fly the first Spitfire to be trained on out of Thame. Officially, we had Sundays off. But I was told if I stayed behind on Sunday, I'd be able to fly one as a trainee.

I spent a lot of time reading the notes beforehand and then I stepped outside to find the Spit waiting for me and a very pleasant senior engineer. My instructor was fretting about the weather. So the engineer took over. He was very calm and collected. I'd already been flying the Hurricane. But this was much better. The Spit is such an easy plane to fly, it's lovely. I went round three times and managed to get down OK. And very soon I was passed out. I had finished my training on the Spitfire.

Then, finally, I could start delivering the planes in earnest. We were issued with overalls to wear. There were two types, a lightweight one and a much heavier overall, both khaki coloured. While we trained, great sheepskin boots were issued to us, as well as a warm padded jacket with a fur collar.

The parachutes we had to take with us were heavy. Once our training was over, there were ATC cadets helping us and sometimes the air crew would help you when you got to the aircraft. It was easiest to put them over your shoulder, rather than carrying them in a bag.

Of course, after having my appendix out, I did find it hard with the parachute and people would say: 'Oh, ask one of the men to help.' But I wouldn't ask. I just hoped someone would offer.

At one point I had to deliver a plane to Dumfries, in Scotland and had to make my way back on the train to London, a very long, slow journey that seemed to take forever. When we finally got there, a man spotted me struggling with my bags and helped me get them off the train. Of course, he wanted to know what was in the heavy bag – it must have looked odd, this small woman, struggling with such a heavy bag.

'Oh it's a parachute,' I explained. Silence. You could see he was taken aback and probably quite puzzled.

The weather was often a problem for us. We had a very good Met officer to check with before we flew out. But you could unexpectedly run into bad weather. Though there were a lot of airfields dotted around the country during the war, so you could land if things got bad, weather wise. Essentially, you just took each day as it came. We were not allowed to fly above 2000ft (600m) and we didn't have radios so it could be quite lonely up there.

I was very lucky. I had aircraft that held together. The worst part was the weather, especially flying when it was hazy. But I was always horrified by the ghastly situations some people would find themselves in – and the wonderful things they did to retrieve the situation. I'd think to myself: 'Now would I have thought of doing that?'

We did have set limits on the hours we could fly but I don't think anyone stuck by them. You just flew the planes until you couldn't fly any more. Most of the aircraft were priority, anyway, so if you thought you could manage it, you kept going. The further you got with the types of planes you flew, the more valuable you were.

I didn't have any accidents but there was one plane I had a problem with, a Barracuda. It was the only time I was asked to ferry a plane to the Isle of Man. Just as I was flying over Douglas, there was an almighty bang. I'd closed the throttle and the engine was still running but there was a tremendous vibration. I decided to try to land in an airfield. Something must have broken. Luckily, I came in OK on the right side of the runway. I got there. But it was a very unpleasant incident.

Then, one time when I had to collect a Barracuda in East Anglia, I had another problem. The plane had a break handle, which meant you could put the seat up or down. I had let the seat down and put it up again but just when I was taking off, halfway up the runway, the seat went down. I could just about see over the rim of the thing and as I was flying across country I knew quite well, I managed quite nicely. But I never ever touched the seat again after that.

When I got my two days off, I'd go and sit with my father. It gave me a chance to talk to him. But he was weakening. For months we'd tried to get Bobby back from Egypt on compassionate leave so he could see him and by now, my father was really only managing to keep going with the help of some medication.

It was all very sad and difficult, especially for my mother. But the life I was leading was a strange life, in many ways; it wasn't something my parents could understand. Some people from ATA would go up to London on their days off, but I never did that. I'd had a few passing boyfriends in my time as a Wren, but nothing really deep. And once I was flying, I was so busy with the work, the planes, I didn't have time to think about having a social life. Two of my male friends had been killed quite early on in the war. That was a blow too. But mostly, when you were flying, you were totally absorbed in it all. At the end of the working day, you'd usually be exhausted.

After several months, I was sent to a billet at Cookham so I could fly out of HQ at White Waltham for my conversion course, training to fly Class 3 planes, the Oxford and the Anson. We trained on the Oxford. I was billeted with a husband and wife; he was a retired Navy commander who had gone into the RAF. They had two sons. One was away at the time at prep school. But their eldest boy had gone into the RAF – and had been killed in a Spitfire accident not long before I arrived.

We became good friends after that and much later, they told me I'd turned up in their lives at just the right time, it was something else to focus on after getting such bad news. And I was a girl, which made a real difference to them. It was a really strong friendship. Many years later, we'd go sailing together down at the Isle of Wight and I would crew for their younger son on his boat.

Back at Hamble, I carried on ferrying the planes until the war ended. I finished at Hamble in September 1945. I was very sad. It was a most peculiar feeling, handing everything in, winding it all up.

On one of my last ever Spitfire deliveries to a depot in Scotland, I expressed my feelings in words. On our chits for each delivery we made there was a section where you wrote down any comments you might have. This particular Spitfire had belonged to the Fleet Air Arm. I had to collect it for the last time ever from Henstridge, near Dorset. They were very upset to hand it over. We all knew she was going to be broken up. So I wrote on my chit: 'This is a beautiful aeroplane and should not be broken up.'

Now it was all over. My friends at Cookham helped me with my luggage and drove me home to Sussex on that last day. At home, things were not good. My father was gone. Fortunately, my brother Bobby had managed to get special leave to come home to see him and my father died a week later, very peacefully. Then my mother had moved to another house 15 miles east of Pulborough, a place called Henfield. So the war was over. And everything was now quite different.

I tried my best to take up village life again, get the house straight, but my father's death seemed to have affected everything. There was a cottage in the garden of the Henfield house and we wound up living in both houses for a time. And we started to keep bulldogs, which was a great distraction for my mother.

Fortunately, I did manage to keep flying for a while after the war, training with the volunteer reserves at a private landing ground near Hatfield until they closed the reservist pool down. I did that on weekends for two weeks a year. I did my instrument rating there. In ATA, of course, we were not trained to fly on instruments.

In 1950 I went to Bermuda with some naval friends for nearly six months. It was the hottest summer they'd had there for ages. Everyone was playing canasta, which was the new thing at the time. But there wasn't very much to do there. So I was really happy when I discovered I could actually pay to fly a seaplane there. I couldn't resist it. I went up three or four times. I went solo once, then I took a friend each time. It was glorious.

But after that, I didn't fly any more. I couldn't really afford it and fortunately, I had developed a real interest in sailing, so that was a weekend pastime. Later in 1950, I started to work in London as a secretary in what was then the War Office and is now the Ministry of Defence. At first I worked at a Fighter Control Unit at Queen Anne Square.

In London, I'd rent a small flat or bedsitter and go home to the countryside to see my mother on weekends. At one point I lived in a big house in Chelsea, a house full of bedsits with a shared bathroom. I did like working in the War Office. I didn't feel I could leave my mother on her own all the time and it suited me to have the job. But I often thought I'd have liked to have gone as a cook with a sailing club on our long holiday breaks; at the War Office we got five weeks holiday a year.

When she died in 1960, my mother left me the cottage. So I continued to live there on weekends, working in London during the week. My work was connected with defence, so it was tied up with security. And, of course, working with the services is mostly confidential work. But by the mid 1970s, I was tired, tension that had been building up for years. I'd always had back trouble, it began in my twenties – I fell off a horse – then my neck and shoulders got worse.

I had very little money at the time but one day, while on leave from work, I made a big decision. I knew I could sell the cottage in Sussex, as prices were starting to rise then. I'd done 23 years in my job. I was ready to retire. I decided to move to Wales, to a cottage in a little village near Lampeter in Ceredigion. I'd bought the cottage with a friend years before. She was another ex-Wren and she and her husband had been using it mostly on weekends while I got there whenever I could. So in the end, I bought her out.

In one way, I was sorry to leave Sussex after so many years. My brother Bobby had married in 1950 and moved to Redhill with his wife, though they didn't have children and he died in the late 1970s.

I had loved the Wales cottage right from the moment I first saw it and I thought 'I've got to come and live here.' When the furniture removal people turned up to move my belongings into the cottage in Wales, it wasn't quite ready for me to move into. A little man from Pickfords came down from Aberystwyth and said to me: 'Oh, you've left a very nice house in England,' meaning the cottage looked shocking, cracked windows, very rundown. But I got it all done eventually.

I'd left behind a very busy life in London and I knew it was going to be very different here in Wales. But luckily, that first summer when I moved in was lovely. Petrol was only beginning to go up, from 30p to 70p a gallon, which seemed shocking at the time. I spent that summer travelling around, exploring places. Friends came to stay. And despite my back problem, I found I could dig across the garden – just under 5 acres – and there's a field across the road with wild flowers, which is so pretty. So I dug and I planted. And I knew then I'd made the right decision to come here.

Gradually I got to know people. This is a Welsh speaking area. Yet they welcomed me in the village, people were very kind to me when I first settled here. But I did keep quiet about the flying when I came here. Very few people knew about it. I thought it might be unpopular because I'm a woman. Now, of course, I realise I was wrong. That wasn't the case at all.

Now, I look back and see that the ATA years were an amazing time, such a different world that we lived in. And of course, over the years, I've remained in touch with many of my ATA friends and colleagues and will still get to reunions if I can organise it. Everyone around me supports me now that I'm getting old. So I'm very, very lucky in that too.

You never really forget it all. But the funny thing was, afterwards, I never really wanted to be flown by anyone. Some years ago, I was in a plane coming from Scotland and we were just coming into Heathrow. There wasn't much wind and the pilot was obviously trying to get the speed down a bit. But he was a bit slow in getting the throttle open a bit and we got what is called an air pocket – but it isn't really, it's because you've lost speed.

I couldn't help it. My right arm shot forward, much to the amusement of the person in the next seat. I'd just anticipated it automatically.

Flying Spitfires was a wonderful experience. But flying all those other planes was wonderful too. It's marvellous to get the recognition, though all the attention on the women does tend to ignore the men who flew for the ATA: some of them were heavily disabled, two had one eye and one arm – yet they flew.

I'd imagine some of the original girls who started it all would turn in their graves now at all the fuss. After the war, people just went their own way, got on with their lives. We just did what was needed at the time, really.

Appendix I

RANKS OF THE ATA

Commodore   reserved to Commanding Officer, ATA
(1 plain wide patch 2in x 2½in)

Senior Commander   reserved to certain of the most senior
executives (4 broad stripes)

Commander   reserved to certain senior executives and the
Officers commanding major Pools (3 broad
stripes)

Captain   reserved to certain executive heads, Officers,
Commanding lesser Pools and seconds-
in-command major Pools (1 broad stripe,
2 narrow, 1 broad)

Flight Captain   reserved to pilots and others in charge of
flights and/or holding positions of authority
or responsibility, requiring seniority
provided by this rank (1 broad stripe,
1 narrow, 1 broad)

1st Officer	available to pilots having at least Class 5 qualifications or to pilots who have been 2nd Officers for at least eighteen months and have attained at least Class 4 qualifications (2 broad stripes)
2nd Officer	available to suitable pilots having at least Class 4 qualifications, and ground staff of equivalent status (1 broad stripe, 1 narrow)
3rd Officer	available to suitable Class 2 and 3 pilots and ground staff of equivalent status (1 broad stripe)
Cadet	A pilot under instruction (1 narrow stripe)

All stripes in gold. Distinctive background as follows:

Flying staff (on pilots' contract)	Dark Blue
Operations staff (including Operations Adjutant)	White
Administrative staff & Adjutants	Green
Flight Engineers, Technical and MT staff	Purple
Medical	Red

Appendix II

ATA FERRY PILOTS AND FLIGHT ENGINEERS

Ferry Pilots

AGAZARIAN, Monique, 3rd Officer, joined on 18.10.43, left on
30.9.45

ALEXANDER, S.M.A., 3rd Officer, joined on 8.5.44, left on
30.9.45

ALLEN, Mrs J.M., 1st Officer, joined on 15.7.42, left on 30.9.45

ALLEN, Myrtle R., 2nd Officer, joined on 12.8.42, left on 1.2.44

ALLEN, Mrs Naomi, 1st Officer, joined on 24.2.42, left on
31.10.45

ANDERSON, Mrs O.P.L., 1st Officer, joined on 10.6.42, left on
9.4.45

ARKLESS, Irene, 2nd Officer, killed on 3.1.43

ARTHUR, J.H., 3rd Officer, joined on 8.5.44, left on 30.9.45

BAINES, R.P., 3rd Officer, joined on 28.12.43, left on 30.9.45

BALLARD, Mrs Ruth E., 1st Officer, joined on 25.6.40, left on
23.1.45

BANNISTER, Mrs E.R., 3rd Officer, joined on 12.7.43, left on 30.9.45

BARNATO WALKER, Mrs Diana, 1st Officer, joined on 2.12.41 left on 31.8.45

BEAUMONT, Edith, 3rd Officer, joined on 20.9.44, left on 30.9.45

BENNETT, Mrs Faith, 1st Officer, joined on 8.7.41, left on 31.7.45

BENNETT, Philippa, Flight Captain, joined on 26.6.40, left on 30.11.45

BEVERLEY, Mrs Patricia, 1st Officer, joined on 29.7.42, left on 31.10.45

BIRD, Jean, 1st Officer, joined on 1.8.41, left on 30.11.45

BLACK, Betty E. (New Zealand), 1st Officer, joined on 15.4.42, left on 30.9.45

BLACKWELL, Mrs P. Ann, 1st Officer, joined on 24.2.42, left on 31.12.45

BONNETT, Mrs R.L., 3rd Officer, joined on 21.2.44, left on 30.9.45

BRAGG, Mrs Dorothy Rita, 1st Officer, joined on 10.2.42, left on 7.6.44

BRAGG, Mrs Felicity. Captain, joined on 1.5.41, left on 30.9.45

BROAD, Jennie, 1st Officer, joined on 30.7.40, left on 11.6.43

BUTLER, Mrs Lois, 1st Officer, joined on l5.2.40, left on 31.5.45

CHAPIN, Emily, 2nd Officer, joined on 18.8.42, left on 11.2.44

CHAPMAN, Susan P., 3rd Officer, joined on 21.2.44, left on 30.9.45

CHOLMONDELEY, Victoria (Australia), 1st Officer, joined on 10.3.41, left on 30.11.45

CLAYTON, Mrs E.V. 'Sammy', 2nd Officer, joined on 1.3.41, left on 20.2.42

COCHRAN-ODLUM, Mrs J. Hon., Flight Captain, joined on 24.1.42, left on 2.7.42

CRIPPS, Mrs B.P. (South Africa), 3rd Officer, joined on 14.6.43, left on 30.9.45

CROSSLEY, Fidelia, 2nd Officer, joined on 16.12.40, left on 26.1.42

CUNNINGTON, Joan, 3rd Officer, joined on 1.6.43, left on 13.9.44

CURTIS, Lettice, 1st Officer, joined on 6.7.40, left on 30.11.45

DAAB, Mrs Anna (Poland), 1st Officer, joined on 6.1.41, left on 30.11.45

DAVISON, Mrs Joy, 2nd Officer, killed on 25.5.40

DE BUNSEN, Mary, 1st Officer, joined on 1.8.41, left on 31.8.45

DE NEVE, Mrs Aimee, 3rd Officer, joined on 8.5.44, left on 30.9.45.

DOUGLAS, Mrs Anne C., 1st Officer, joined on 1.12.40, left on 19.8.42

DUHALDE, Margot (Chile), 1st Officer, joined on 1.9.41, left on 30.11.45

DUNLOP, Maureen A.C., 1st Officer, joined on l5.4.42, left on 30.11.45

DUTTON, Joan (The Hon. Mrs), 1st Officer, joined on 1.3.41, left on 30.11.45

EBBAGE, Mrs Margaret, Flight Captain, joined on 1.1.40, left on 23.3.43

EDWARDS, Mrs Sylvia I., 2nd Officer, joined on 9.8.43, left on 30.9.45

EVELEIGH, Mrs Y.M., 3rd Officer, joined on 21.2.44, left on 30.9.45

EVERARD-STEENKAMP, Mrs Rosamund, 2nd Officer, killed on 19.1.46, the last ATA pilot to be killed

FAHIE, Mrs Pauline, Senior Commander, joined on 1.12.39, left on 31.10.45

FAIR, Mrs Winifred, Flight Captain, joined on 1.1.40, left on 30.11.45

FAIRWEATHER, Margaret, Flight Captain, joined on 1.1.40, killed on 4.8.44

FALKNER, Lucy, Flight Captain, joined on 1.4.41, left on 31.12.45

FARNELL, Mrs Diane, 2nd Officer, joined on 16.9.40, left on 25.3.42

FARR, Virginia, 1st Officer, joined on 10.2.42, left on 5.6.45

FARQUHAR, Marjory J., 3rd Officer, joined on 22.1.44, left on 30.9.45

FAUNETHORPE, Diana, 3rd Officer, joined on 21.2.44, left on 30.9.45

FERGUSON, Joy, 2nd Officer, joined on 1.5.43, left on 31.10.45

FORD, Mrs Mary E., 1st Officer, joined on 10.6.42, left on 2.9.44

FORD, Suzanne H., 1st Officer, joined on l4.4.42, left on 31.10.45

FORWARD, Mrs Mona, 1st Officer, joined on 1.1.40, left on 29.2.43

FROST, Margaret, 3rd Officer, joined on 25.11.42, left on 30.9.45

GARRETT, Mrs Sheila, 3rd Officer, joined on 3.3.44, left on 30.6.45

GARST, Virginia, 3rd Officer, joined on 14.4.42, left on 24.11.42

GETHIN, Mrs Margaret, 1st Officer, joined on 12.8.42, left on 17.9.44

GLASS, Mabel, 1st Officer, joined on 8.7.40, left on 17.4.44

GOLLAN, Mrs Pamela, 1st Officer, joined on 15.8.41, left on 15.8.44

GOODWIN, Una, Cadet, joined on 10.6.42, left on 2.9.42

GORE, Margot, Commander, joined on 25.6.40, left on 30.11.45

GOUGH, Joyce, 3rd Officer, joined on 28.12.43, left on 30.9.45

GOWER, Pauline (see Fahie)

GUTHRIE, Mary, 3rd Officer, joined on 18.10.43, left on 30.9.45

HANSEN-LESTER, Mrs D.E., 2nd Officer, joined on 23.9.42, left on 13.2.44

HARRISON, Mrs Helen M., 1st Officer, joined on 1.5.42, left on 23.3.44

HAYMAN, Mrs Beatrice, 1st Officer, joined on 16.12.41, left on 30.11.45

HENNINGS, Sophie E.V.A., 3rd Officer, joined on 29.11.43, left on 25.4.45

HEPPELL, Rhoda, 3rd Officer, joined on 16.12.41, left on 31.7.42

HILL, Bridget G.M.L., 3rd Officer, killed on 15.3.42

HIRSCH, Mrs K.M.S., 3rd Officer, joined on 8.5.44, left on 30.9.45

HORSBURGH, Mrs Francis, 3rd Officer, joined on 21.2.44, left on 27.4.45

HOWDEN, June C., 3rd Officer, joined on 6.12.43, left on 12.5.45

HUDSON, Evelyn, 1st Officer, joined 10.6.41, left on 19.8.43

HUGHES, Joan, Flight Captain, joined on 1.1.40, left on 31.12.45

HUNTER, Mrs Mary, 1st Officer, joined on 1.3.41, left on 6.5.43

HUNTER, Trevor, 1st Officer, joined on 20.11.41, left on 31.7.45

ILLSLEY, Mrs K.D., 1st Officer, joined on 1.9.41, left on 30.11.45

IRWIN, Mrs Zita, 1st Officer, joined on 15.8.41, left on 30.11.45

JENNER, Zoe, 3rd Officer, joined on 6.9.43, left on 30.9.45

JOHNSON, Amy (Mrs Amy Mollison) 1st Officer killed on 5.1.41

KEITH-JOPP, Betty, 3rd Officer, joined on 8.5.44, left on 17.8.45

KERLY, Ruth, 3rd Officer, joined on 23.8.43, left on 30.9.45

LANG, Mrs Dora, 1st Officer, killed on 2.3.44

LANKSHEAR, Barbara L., 3rd Officer, joined on 21.12.44, left on 30.9.45

LARGE, Gloria, Cadet, joined on 5.7.42, left on 21.9.42

LEAF, Freydis, 1st Officer, joined on 17.2.43, left on 31.10.45

LEATHART, Constance R., Flight Captain, joined on l4.8.40, left on 30.6.44

LENNOX, Mrs Margaret, 1st Officer, joined on 10.6.42, left on 30.11.45

LESTER, Mrs K.M., 3rd Officer, joined on 14.6.43, left on 28.2.45

LOVELL-PANK, Mrs J.A., 3rd Officer, joined on 15.11.43, left on 14.8.45

MACDONALD, Mrs Yvonne, 3rd Officer, joined on 6.9.43, left on 30.6.45

MACDOUGALL, Elizabeth, 2nd Officer, joined on 16.9.42, left on 23.8.45

MACKENZIE, Mrs Audrey, 1st Officer, joined on 26.6.40, left on 8.8.45

MACLEOD, Mrs Rosemary T., 3rd Officer, joined on 7.6.43, left on 16.4.45

MAHON, Mrs Annette E., 3rd Officer, joined on 8.5.44, left on 30.9.45

MARSHALL, Joan, 3rd Officer, killed on 19.6.42

MAY, The Hon. Elizabeth, Flight Captain, joined on 1.3.41, left on 30.8.45

METCALFE, Mrs Ursula, 1st Officer, joined on 23.6.40, left on 16.10.43

MILLER, Nancy, 1st Officer, joined on 9.7.42, left on 8.7.45

MILSTEAD, Violet, 1st Officer, joined on 5.5.43, left on 31.7.45

MOGGRIDGE, Mrs Dolores T., 1st Officer, joined on 31.7.40, left on 30.11.45

MOORE, The Hon. Mrs Ruth, 1st Officer, joined on 15.4.41, left on 17.4.43

MORGAN, Audrey, 3rd Officer, joined on 6.9.43, left on 30.9.45

MULLINEAUX, Joan E.F., 3rd Officer, joined on 1.5.43, left on 30.9.45

MURRAY, Leslie, 3rd Officer, killed on 20.4.45

NAYLER, Joan E., 1st Officer, joined on 16.12.41, left on 31.12.45

NICHOLSON, Mary W., 2nd Officer, killed on 22.5.43

OBERMER, Ruth, Cadet, joined on 11.10.43, left on 26.6.44

ORR, Mrs Marion, 2nd Officer, joined on 5.4.43, left on 1.10.44

PADDON, Zita, 2nd Officer, joined on 27.8.43, left on 31.10.45

PATTERSON, Mrs Gabrielle, 1st Officer, joined on 1.1.40, left on 23.3.43

PETERSON, Stella J., 3rd Officer, joined on 5.7.43, left on 30.9.45

PIERCE, Winnie R., 1st Officer, joined on 10.2.42, left on 15.5.44

PILSUDSKA, Jadwiga, 2nd Officer, joined on 15.7.42, left on 20.7.44

PLANT, Jane, 1st Officer, joined on 31.3.43, left on 31.10.45

POWER, Cecile, E.R., 2nd Officer, joined on 26.7.43, left on 31.10.45

POWYS, Mary E.A., 3rd Officer, joined on 1.6.43, left on 13.8.45

PROVIS, Patricia M., 3rd Officer, joined on 21.2.44, left on 30.9.45

RAINES, Hazel, 2nd Officer, joined on 14.4.42, left on 24.7.43

RAMSAY, Diana, 1st Officer, joined on 16.12.41, left on 31.7.45

RATCLIFF, Mrs Margaret, 3rd Officer, joined on 10.9.43, left on 30.9.45

REES, Rosemary, Captain, joined on 1.1.40, left on 31.12.45

RICHEY, Helen, 1st Officer, joined on 25.3.42, left on 20.1.43

RHONIE, A.H., 3rd Officer, joined on 30.11.43, left on 19.11.44

ROSE, Mrs Mollie, 1st Officer, joined on 16.9.42, left on 25.5.45

ROWLAND, Mrs Marigold, 2nd Officer, joined on 1.5.43, left on 24.4.5

RUMBALL, Mrs Daphne A., 3rd Officer, joined on 25.5.43, left on 31.5.45

RUSSELL, Margaret E., 2nd Officer, joined on 25.9.43, left on 31.10.45

RUSSELL, Ruth M.H., 3rd Officer, joined on 21.2.44, left on 30.9.45

SALE-BARKER, Audrey D., 1st Officer, joined on 26.6.40, left on 30.11.45

SALMON, Mrs Honour I.P., 1st Officer, killed on 19.4.43

SANDOZ-LEVEAUX, Mrs R.B., 2nd Officer, joined on 12.8.42, left on 11.2.44

SAYER, Betty E., Cadet, killed on l5.3.42

SCHUURMANN, Louise E.M., 1st Officer, joined on 10.2.42, left on 30.6.45

SHARPE, Roy M., 1st Officer, joined on 3.9.41, left on 30.9.45

SHARPE, Ethel E., 3rd Officer, joined on 1.11.43, left on 15.6.45

SHIEL, Maureen E., 3rd Officer, joined on 20.9.43, left on 31.8.45

SLADE, Eleanor 'Susan', Flight Captain, killed on 13.7.44

SMITH, Diana P.M., 1st Officer, joined on 7.10.42, left on 31.10.45

STEARNS, Mrs Edith, 1st Officer, joined on 10.6.42, left on 9.6.45

STEVENSON, Grace, 1st Officer, joined on 14.4.42, left on 13.4.45

STOKES, Winifred, 3rd Officer, joined on 21.2.44, left on l4.4.45

STRODL, Vera E., 1st Officer, joined on 2.12.41, left on 30.11.45

THARP, Mrs Joyce A., 3rd Officer, joined on 21.2.44, left on 14.4.45

TULK-Hart, Pamela, 3rd Officer, joined on 25.8.42, left on 31.8.45

VAN DOOZER, Catherine, 2nd Officer, joined on 9.6.42, left on 31.3.44

VAN ZANTEN, Ida L.V., 3rd Officer, joined on 18.5.43, left on 30.9.45

VOLKERSZ, Mrs Veronica, Flight Captain, joined on 1.3.41, left on 30.11.45

WADSWORTH, Eleanor D., 3rd Officer, joined on 1.6.43, left on 30.9.45

WALKER, Anne, 1st Officer, joined on 17.7.42, left on 31.10.45

WHITTALL, Taniya, 2nd Officer, killed on 8.4.44

WILBERFORCE, Mrs Marion K. Commander, joined on 1.1.40, left on 7.8.45

WILKINS, Mary (Mary Ellis), 1st Officer, joined on 1.10.41, left on 31.12.45

WILLIS, Mrs Benedetta, 1st Officer, joined on 1.9.41, left on 3.8.43

WILSON, Mrs Irene M.E., 2nd Officer, joined on 1.6.43, left on 31.10.45

WINSTONE, Jane, 2nd Officer, killed on 10.2.44

WITHERBY, Mrs Joan D., 2nd Officer, joined on 17.6.42, left on 29.5.45

WOOD, Ann W., 1st Officer, joined on 29.4.42, left on 30.11.45

WOJTULANIS, Stefania, 1st Officer, joined on 1.1.41, left on 4.5.45

WYNNE-EYTON, Mrs Helen, 1st Officer, joined on 1.11.40, left on 28.10.43

Flight Engineers

HARRINGTON, Janice, Flight Engineer, killed on 2.3.44

PARKER, Patricia M.B., 3rd Officer/Flight Engineer, joined on 30.4.41, left on 31.12.44

PIERCE, Mrs Phyllis O., Flight Engineer, joined on 26.10.43, left on 23.4.44

THOMAS, Mrs Barbara, 3rd Officer/Flight Engineer, joined on 19.4.43, left on 31.7.45

Source: *The Forgotten Pilots* by Lettice Curtis

Appendix III

FIVE LIVES LOST

Sixteen female ATA pilots and one flight engineer lost their lives during the Second World War. As Mary (Wilkins) Ellis described it so poignantly, the unexpected loss of a colleague was a bitter blow. While this was not a common occurrence at the women's ferry pools, each time there was a fatality, everyone fervently hoped it would be the last.

Here are brief histories of five ATA women who paid the ultimate price for their courage at different stages of the war.

Elsie Davison

Elsie Davison was the first female ATA pilot to lose her life. Born in Toronto, Canada, in 1910, Elsie Muntz learned to fly at age 20. Emigrating with her family to England, she married businessman Frank Davison in 1933 and the couple ran a small aviation company called Utility Airways in Cheshire.

One of the ATA's earliest ferry pilots, in the spring of 1940 she wrote to a relative describing her work as 'extremely dangerous now and I don't know whether I will come out of it.'

It was a tragic prophesy. On 25 May 1940, Elsie and her instructor were killed during a training flight at RAF Upavon, Wiltshire. It is believed that carbon monoxide leaked into the cockpit of their plane, rendering them unconscious and causing the plane to crash.

Jane Winstone

Born in Wanganui, New Zealand in 1912, Jane Winstone took up flying as a schoolgirl. She won her pilot's licence at age nineteen, flying in many air pageants around New Zealand. Following Jean Batten's record-breaking flight from England to Australia in 1934, she made a tour of New Zealand. Jane Winstone and three other women pilots flew to meet Batten in their Gypsy Moths to accompany her to Wanganui.

Keen to get involved with the war effort, Jane applied to fly with the ATA and was accepted in 1942. In June that year, just before she was scheduled to leave New Zealand for England, she received bad news: her fiancé, Angus Carr MacKenzie, a pilot in the Royal New Zealand Air Force, had been reported missing in a raid over Essen, Germany. His body was never found.

One of five New Zealanders who flew for the ATA during the war, as a 2nd Officer Jane ferried many types of aircraft including Supermarine Spitfires, Hawker Hurricanes and Gloster Gladiators.

By early 1944 she was based at the all-women's ferry pool at Cosford. On 10 February that year she was taking off in a Spitfire and the engine failed at 600ft. The plane spun into the ground and Jane was killed, aged 31. After the war, fellow New Zealand ATA pilot 1st Officer Trevor Hunter returned Jane's logbooks to her family in New Zealand.

Amy Johnson

Her name instantly resonates as a pioneer of aviation. Amy Johnson became a worldwide celebrity in the years before the Second World War – and an inspiration to many thousands of young women who dreamed of taking to the skies.

Born in 1903, her father owned a fish processing business in Hull. Rebellious at school, she graduated from Sheffield University and took up flying as a hobby, eventually persuading her father to help buy her a De Havilland Moth. In 1930, she became a global superstar as the first woman to fly solo to Australia. A brilliant and courageous flyer, after that epic flight her name was rarely out of the newspaper headlines.

By the outbreak of war, she was divorced from her husband, Scottish aviator Jim Mollison and her hopes of playing a major role in advising the aviation authorities in wartime remained unrealised. Nonetheless, head of the ATA's women's section, Pauline Gower, invited Amy to join the ATA and in July 1940 she started work as a ferry pilot at Hatfield.

Early in January 1941, Amy travelled up to Prestwick to collect an Oxford aircraft to be flown to RAF Kidlington, near Oxford. But the wintry bad weather and heavy cloud meant she had to put down at Blackpool, where she remained overnight. She took off the next day and headed south on 5 January.

Yet again, she ran into dense cloud. Then the Oxford ran out of fuel. Amy managed to parachute out of the plane into the Thames Estuary, near Herne Bay, Kent and was spotted by the crew of a naval trawler who immediately altered course.

Although they bravely attempted to rescue Amy, the seas were rough with a heavy swell and she failed to catch the ropes that were thrown out to her. It is believed she was sucked down into the ship's propellers.

Amy Johnson's body was never recovered, leading to any number of theories and rumours about her death, including suicide and a mysterious 'passenger' in the Oxford. Sadly, the man who attempted to rescue Britain's most brilliant female aviator, Lt Commander Walter Fletcher, who had dived into the water to help her, lost his life too in heavy seas.

Dora Lang and Janice Harrington

Dora and Janice were killed on 2 March 1944 when the Mosquito they were travelling in from Lasham, Hants, crashed on landing. An accomplished pilot, 1st Officer Dora Lang, a married woman from London in her late twenties, had joined the ATA in 1941. Flight Engineer Janice Harrington, 23, had hoped to be a pilot. But she was not accepted for ATA flight training because she was not tall enough.

A schoolteacher, she then spent all her free time studying engineering and when it was agreed that women flight engineers could be accepted into the ATA, Janice applied and was promptly accepted.

A beautiful young woman, in 1943 her portrait was painted by the well known artist Harold Speed and hung in the Royal Academy. Harold Speed is reported to have said he considered her one of the most beautiful girls he had ever met.

The following extract from *Golden Wings*, the story of some of the women's ferry pilots of the ATA, was written by Alison King, who worked as an ATA Operations Officer at Hamble. The book was published in 1954. The extract tells of the impact of the news of the Mosquito crash on the women's ferry pool on that day in 1944.

Came a sunny day in 1944 with the programme not weighty but full enough – the weather good – a reasonably leisurely day – a happy day. Veronica had taken the Anson, Anna and 5 others were flying Spitfires to Shawbury. Dora and one of the women flight engineers had taken a Hudson to Cosford, with a Mosquito back to Lasham, and Grace the American had a duplicate trip. We were getting through well, the first trips had been made, and the pilots were well on with their second deliveries, lunch was over and a few were sitting round, preparatory to starting on their new job.

A pilot or two were sitting round, looking out of place as they somehow did in a women's Mess.

I was checking some papers as Rachel stretched her arm out to answer the phone. Not really listening, nevertheless I heard a desultory conversation and perceptively a change of voice. I looked up quickly to see Rachel with a face grown old and grey.

'Dora,' she mouthed at me, while still listening. So apparent was the tragedy in her face that I knew so much but not all. I steeled myself for the necessary question.

'Dead?' I whispered.

She nodded. 'And the flight engineer … and Janice?' I asked.

She turned again to the phone and asked this question, then with a curiously helpless twist of the hand, she turned back to me.

'Both,' she mouthed. Sickness welled in the pit of my stomach…

Later we learned that the first Mosquito having landed, the second which was very close behind, had made a circuit and started quite normally on its approach. Then, when it was only about twenty feet over the runway, it suddenly reared up, turned on its back and dived into the ground. There was no hope at all and the horrified onlookers could do nothing. It was never really discovered exactly what could have happened to make a brilliant pilot and a beautifully designed aircraft perish almost at the point of a normal landing. The Accident Investigation people never produced any particular finding, although there were many theories …

I had already altered the huge blackboard that hung down one side of the room.

It bore the names of the pilots and their leave for the month. If someone was killed, no gaps were left, the name was erased and everyone else moved up – quickly …

Appendix IV

FAMOUS PILOTS OF THE ATA

Pauline Gower, MBE
'Every Woman Should Learn To Fly'

Pauline Mary de Peauly Gower was born in 1910, one of two daughters of Sir Robert Gower, Conservative MP for Gillingham, Kent. Educated at the Convent of the Sacred Heart in Tunbridge Wells, she fell seriously ill as a teenager: pneumonia and pleurisy, together with a bad ear infection, followed by surgery. It was touch and go for a while but she rallied – though future sporting activities were forbidden.

Energetic and bright, she turned to the idea of flying and took her first flight whilst still at school. Then, after finishing school in Paris and being presented at Court, she decided to learn to fly in 1930, without telling her parents.

While learning to fly, she teamed up with another flying devotee, Dorothy Spicer, and the pair conceived a plan: they'd go into the flying business. Pauline would be a commercial pilot and Dorothy would qualify as a flight engineer.

In 1931, newly qualified and having purchased a two-seater plane called a Spartan, the two women started to run joyrides from a small field alongside a main road in Kent.

After this, they joined air circuses, initially a small one in 1931, then a larger one employing fifteen pilots and three parachutists. This proved very successful for the Spicer-Gower team: that year they flew over 6000 passengers.

In 1934, they started a joy riding business in a field near Hunstanton, Norfolk. They charged passengers £1 for a 40-mile round 'taxi' trip to Skegness. A year later, they'd formed Air Trips Limited, returning to flying circus work again with Campbell Black's Air Display during the following year.

It was a peripatetic way of life and the English weather was a constant source of frustration. Following an accident in Coventry and a stint in hospital – Pauline's plane was hit by another aircraft on take off – the novelty of the flying circus work had worn thin for her. In those years, she had carried over 33,000 passengers. She had also made her mark in aviation history: the country's first-ever female commercial aviator. Not surprisingly, her passion for aviation remained undiminished.

On the ground, and with war on the horizon, she started to use her skills in a new direction, working with the Civil Air Guard as a Defence Commissioner for London, lecturing to encourage other women to fly and using her contacts and background to encourage the authorities to allow women to fly during wartime. All this led to her appointment as head of the women's section of the ATA in 1939.

In 1943, she was appointed to the board of the newly reformed BOAC. In June of that year, the ATA women pilots were awarded equal pay with the men: a remarkable achievement that can only be attributed to Pauline Gower's efforts on behalf of the women.

In 1944, she married Wing Commander Bill Fahie. Tragically, in 1947, at the age of 36, she died giving birth to twin sons, a premature end to a remarkable life.

Diana Barnato Walker, MBE
The Legendary Debutante

Born in 1918 into a wealthy family, Diana and her sister Virginia grew up in some splendour, surrounded by servants, in a large house in London's Primrose Hill. At age four, their parents split up, though remaining on good terms, so that Diana would frequently join her racing car driving father Woolf Barnato at his magnificent home in Surrey (often described as 'more like the Savoy than home'), scene of lavish entertainments and wild all-night parties.

After leaving Queen's College, Diana came out as a debutante in 1936 and was presented at Court. But she had already been bitten by the flying bug, spending her pocket money on flying lessons at Brooklands in a Tiger Moth. (On the day of her flying test, she is reputed to have turned up in an expensive leopard skin coat belonging to her stepmother, claiming she had no other coat, and for her 21st birthday she was given a Bentley by her father.)

When war was declared in September 1939, she initially volunteered to join the Red Cross but then applied to the ATA as a ferry pilot, joining the ATA in December 1941. By the age of 23 she was delivering Spitfires – and had experienced a series of death defying incidents in the air. Claiming to have a 'guardian angel', a badly burned man she had met on her first solo flight at Brooklands who had said, 'Don't fly, Miss Barnato, look what it's done to me,' she insisted that after that she was always a careful pilot.

Engaged to dashing fighter ace Squadron Leader Humphrey Gilbert in 1942, she learned just a few days after their official engagement that he had been killed flying a Spitfire. She married Wing Commander Derek Walker in 1944. He too was killed in 1945 whilst flying to a job interview in a Mustang.

She obtained a commercial air licence after the war and became Corps Pilot for the Women's Junior Air Corps, encouraging a generation of young women to consider working in aviation.

In 1963, aged 45, she became the first British woman to break the sound barrier, flying a supersonic Lightning T4 for the RAF. Continuing to fly with the WJAC, she became Commodore of the ATA Association and eventually took up sheep farming in Surrey.

For over 30 years she maintained a close relationship with racing driver Whitney Strait and the pair had a son, Barney, born in 1947. Diana never wished for Strait to leave his wife. 'I had my own identity,' she said later. 'I was perfectly content.'

In 1994, her memoir *Spreading My Wings* was published and, aged 88, she took the controls of her last Spitfire. She died in 2008, aged 90.

Lettice Curtis
The ATA Superstar

Born in Devon on 1 February 1916, the daughter of a country lawyer, Lettice was educated at Benenden School, Kent, where she became School Captain. In 1933, she completed her education at St Hilda's College, Oxford, studying maths and becoming Captain of the University's Women's Lawn Tennis and Fencing teams, learning to fly at Yapton Flying Club at Ford, West Sussex, in 1938. She had been working as a pilot for a survey company in 1940 when she decided to join the ATA.

In her five-year wartime career with the ATA, she flew an extraordinary number of different types of aircraft and was one of the first women to qualify to fly heavy bombers, eventually ferrying over 330 four-engined bombers. She was the first woman to deliver a Lancaster.

After the war she worked as a technician and test flight observer at the A & AEE (Aeroplane and Armament Experimental Establishment) the military aircraft test establishment at Boscombe Down in Wiltshire.

Following this she was a Senior Flight Development Engineer with Fairey Aviation, flying the company's communication aircraft. She also took an active part in air racing, flying her own Foster Wikner Wicko and a Spitfire owned by the US attaché in London.

After leaving Fairey Aviation in the 1960s she worked for many years for the Ministry of Aviation, working on the initial planning of the joint Civil/RAF Air Traffic Control Centre at West Drayton, then working in the Flight Operations Inspectorate for the CAA until 1976.

She formally retired in 1979 after a period working as an engineer for Sperry's in Bracknell, Berks. She continued to fly until nearly eighty, qualifying as a helicopter pilot in 1992. She finally stopped flying in 1995. She died, aged 99, on 21 July 2014.

Monique Agazarian
The Free Spirit

Monique Agazarian's ATA career was followed by a lifetime's career in aviation. And like fellow ATA pilot Mary (Wilkins) Ellis, she is rare in that she went on to run her own successful commercial aviation business after the war.

Petite, dynamic and with an incredible zest for life – on one of her last ATA flights she unofficially flew a naval Seafire at low level over her mother's flat in Knightsbridge on VE Day – she also inspired thousands of would-be pilots through her work as an instructor at her flight training centres at various locations in and around London.

Her book, *Instrument Flying & Background to the IMC Instrument Ratings*, published in 1988, is widely regarded as an important aviation manual on advanced instrument flying procedures.

Born in Surrey in 1920, Monique, the daughter of a French mother and an Armenian father running a successful engineering company, would join her four brothers in childhood games with their favourite 'toy', a First World War Sopwith Pup fighter plane, which her mother had bought at a Croydon auction and installed at the bottom of their garden.

Educated at the Convent of the Sacred Heart, Roehampton, and at a Paris finishing school, after war broke out Monique nursed with the Voluntary Aid Detachment (VAD) at the RAF establishment at Uxbridge. By then, three of her brothers had joined the RAF and Monique was determined to fly.

Early approaches to join the ATA were not successful. She was below minimum height requirement and had no flying experience. Yet somehow she convinced the ATA interviewers to accept her for *ab initio* training at the end of 1943.

Her eldest brother Noel, who had fought in the Battle of Britain, was killed in the Middle East in 1941. Another brother, Jack, was seconded from the RAF to the covert Special Operations Executive as a clandestine wireless operator in France. In July 1943, he had been captured and tortured by the Germans, refusing to reveal any information, only to be executed days before the war ended.

Yet 'Aggie', like many others, did not let personal loss or fear hinder her determination to play her part. She ferried Spitfires, Hurricanes, Seafires, Typhoons and Mustangs for the ATA until the war ended. Then she obtained her commercial pilot's licence.

At first, she joined a company called Island Air Services, set up in June 1945 to fly charter flights out of Elstree and fly flowers from the Scilly Isles to the mainland. By early 1948, Monique had become MD of the company's London operation and in due course IAS was running lucrative joyrides out of Heathrow Airport, Northolt and Croydon for many years, expanding the business in 1950 to fly passengers from Shoreham to Deauville, France, for gambling trips in Deauville's casinos. At one point, two ATA pilots, Veronica Volkersz and Mary Guthrie, flew for Island Air Services.

Monique married fellow pilot Ray Rendall in 1949 and the pair had three daughters, Annette, Mary and Lou-Lou. In 1962, the family moved to Beirut, where Ray flew for Middle East Airlines.

Returning to the UK in 1968, Monique re-started her flying career, initially with charter work and then a part time job with Air Training Services, a company set up to provide *ab initio* flight training in ground simulators, the first of which was set up in the Grosvenor Hotel in London.

In 1976, Monique took over ATS, later moving the business to the Piccadilly Hotel, followed by various moves to other training venues, finally moving to Wycombe Air Park, Booker, in Buckinghamshire, running the ground training centre and simulator until selling the business in 1992. She died in London, aged 72, in 1993.

Maureen Adele Chase Popp (née Dunlop)
The Girl on the Cover

The girl who dazzled the public as the *Picture Post* cover girl was born in 1920 in Buenos Aires, Argentina, to an Australian-born father (who had arrived in Patagonia in 1912, volunteered to fight with the Royal Field Artillery and returned to Patagonia after the war with his English nurse, whom he had married).

Maureen and her sister Joan grew up surrounded by animals in the wide open spaces of Patagonia: Maureen's father had imported sheep from his native New South Wales and worked for the Southern Land Company, managing 250,000 hectares of sheep farms.

Maureen loved horses and flying was a childhood dream. During a holiday in England in 1936 she took flying lessons and when she returned to Argentina she managed to get into a local flying club and continue training. By the age of seventeen she had her pilot's licence.

The Dunlop sisters arrived in England by boat from Buenos Aires in 1940. Maureen intended to fly and Joan to meet her fiance and join the BBC. In April 1942, Maureen joined the ATA, rising through the ranks to 1st Officer and flying thirty-eight different types of aircraft through the war, leaving the ATA in November 1945 to become one of the few ATA female pilots to continue a career in aviation.

Returning to Buenos Aires with Joan, Maureen became a flying instructor in the Argentinian province of Rio Negro, on the northern edge of Patagonia. At one point she was instructing Argentinan Air Force pilots to fly Lancaster bombers, purchased by the Argentinians after the war. She continued to work as a commercial pilot until 1969.

In 1955 she married Serban Popp, a retired Romanian diplomat. The couple went on to have three children. In 1973 the family left for England and a new life involving Maureen's other great passion – breeding Arabian horses. For several years Maureen and Serban ran the Milla Laquen Stud, near Tivetshall, St Margaret, in Norfolk, a stud she had founded in 1947 and brought over to England. After her husband died, Maureen handed on the stud in 2000.

In 2003, Maureen, Lettice Curtis and Diana Barnato-Walker were awarded the Guild of Air Pilots Master Air Pilot Award. Maureen died on 29 May 2012, aged 91.

Joan Hughes, MBE
The 'Baby' of the First Eight

When she retired in 1985, Joan Hughes had clocked up nearly 12,000 flying hours in her logbook. Born in West Ham, London, in 1918, Joan started flying at age fifteen, when she accompanied her older brother to flying lessons. On learning that the lessons would be costing £2 10s an hour, she told her father she so wanted to fly, she was prepared to go without food to do so.

Shortly after going solo, fifteen-year-old Joan's flying had to stop when an accident involving a sixteen-year-old boy pilot led to his death. She resumed flying when a new rule was introduced bringing in a minimum flying age of seventeen – making Joan the youngest female flyer in the country.

With the launch of the Civil Air Guard, she became a civilian flying instructor for three years and was working with fellow 'First Eight' ATA pilot 'Gabby' Patterson at the CAG in Romford when she joined the ATA, the youngest of the first group of women to fly for the ATA.

Tiny in stature, just 5ft 2in, she went on to ferry all types of aircraft for the ATA, including the four-engined bombers, eventually qualifying as the only woman instructor to work on all classes of aircraft. After the war, she continued to work as a flying instructor, eventually working for the Airways Aero Association at Wycombe Air Park.

Thanks to her size and considerable experience she was engaged to fly a replica of a vintage plane (a Demoiselle monoplane) for the 1965 movie, *Those Magnificent Men in their Flying Machines*. Then she appeared in the 1966 movie, *The Blue Max*, flying a First World War replica plane and in 1968, she flew in a Tiger Moth as Lady Penelope's stunt double in the *Thunderbirds* 6 movie. She was acquitted by the authorities in Buckinghamshire for flying too low during the filming of the movie. She retired in 1985 and died in Somerset in 1993 aged 75.

Ann Wood-Kelly
The 'Gal' from Philly

Crossing the Atlantic in a tramp steamer as one of Jackie Cochrane's first group of American women flyers to join the ATA, Ann Wood must have reflected that as the only woman three years before in her flying class in a small university town in Maine, she could never have dreamed she'd be joining the war in Europe – and eventually ferrying Spitfires, Mosquitos and Hawker Hurricanes as a 1st Officer in the ATA.

Born in Philadelphia in 1918 and following several years living in Belgium, where her widowed mother took the family after her husband died, the family returned to the US, where Ann, encouraged by her mother, learned to fly at an otherwise all-male college in Maine. She made her first solo flight after just eight hours' flying.

Not long after receiving her instructors' rating to teach her first civilian pilot's class in 1941, Ann received a very long telegram from Jackie Cochran, asking if she wanted to fly in Britain with the ATA. After meeting with Cochran in New York, Ann was initially turned down as too young and too inexperienced to join Cochran's 'gals'. Yet she eventually found herself on Jackie's team and joined the ATA in April 1942.

During her wartime flying she ferried over 900 planes to England and France, one of a small group of ATA women flyers to fly operational aircraft into France in 1945. That same year she was awarded the King's Medal as an acknowledgement of her contribution to the British war effort.

After the war she initially worked in London as first assistant to the US civil air attaché, returning to work in the US as public relations director for Northeast Airlines, based in Boston. Later she worked for the now defunct Pan American World Airways, eventually becoming Pan Am's first female vice president. For the last decade of her life she travelled across the US lecturing about the wartime work of the ATA.

She continued to fly her Piper Arrow until the age of 87. Her son, Christopher Kelly, recalled her 87th birthday lunch where Ann piloted the flight to Martha's Vineyard. He piloted the plane on the way back. 'But I didn't land as well as she had.' She died in 2006, a month after her 88th birthday.

INDEX

If you enjoyed this book, you may also be interested in...

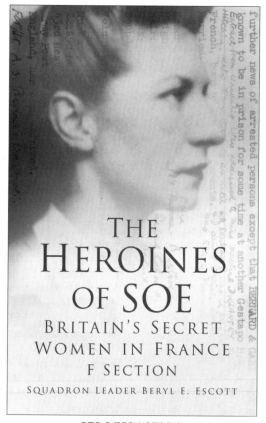

THE
HEROINES
OF SOE
BRITAIN'S SECRET
WOMEN IN FRANCE
F SECTION
SQUADRON LEADER BERYL E. ESCOTT

978 0 7524 8729 8